P9-DVF-729

RENEWALS 458-4574
DATE DUE

GAYLORD   PRINTED IN U.S.A.

WITHDRAWN
UTSA Libraries

Relationship Competence for Healthcare Management

Palgrave Macmillan Studies in Banking and Financial Institutions

Relationship Competence for Healthcare Management

Peer to Peer

Jennifer Landau and Elio Borgonovi

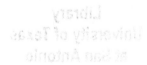

palgrave
macmillan

© Jennifer Landau and Elio Borgonovi 2008

All rights reserved. No reproduction, copy or transmission of this
publication may be made without written permission.

No paragraph of this publication may be reproduced, copied or transmitted
save with written permission or in accordance with the provisions of the
Copyright, Designs and Patents Act 1988, or under the terms of any licence
permitting limited copying issued by the Copyright Licensing Agency, 90
Tottenham Court Road, London W1T 4LP.

Any person who does any unauthorized act in relation to this publication
may be liable to criminal prosecution and civil claims for damages.

The authors have asserted their rights to be identified as the authors
of this work in accordance with the Copyright, Designs and
Patents Act 1988.

First published 2008 by
PALGRAVE MACMILLAN
Houndmills, Basingstoke, Hampshire RG21 6XS and
175 Fifth Avenue, New York, N.Y. 10010
Companies and representatives throughout the world

PALGRAVE MACMILLAN is the global academic imprint of the Palgrave
Macmillan division of St. Martin's Press, LLC and of Palgrave Macmillan Ltd.
Macmillan® is a registered trademark in the United States, United Kingdom
and other countries. Palgrave is a registered trademark in the European
Union and other countries.

ISBN-13: 978–0–230–51596–3   hardback
ISBN-10: 0–230–51596–7   hardback

This book is printed on paper suitable for recycling and made from fully
managed and sustained forest sources. Logging, pulping and manufacturing
processes are expected to conform to the environmental regulations of the
country of origin.

A catalogue record for this book is available from the British Library.

A catalogue record for this book is available from the Library of Congress.

10   9   8   7   6   5   4   3   2   1
17 16 15 14 13 12 11 10 09 08

Printed and bound in Great Britain by
Antony Rowe Ltd, Chippenham and Eastbourne

Library
University of Texas
at San Antonio

For Red, Sacha and Vincent

Contents

List of Figures, Tables and Graphs

Figures

Tables

Graphs

Acknowledgements

A special thank you to Elio's wife Maura and to his daughters Francesca and Veronica for their love and support and to Jennifer's parents Julie and Henry for reading this book over and over again. We would also like to thank Nezha Aharas, Amelia Compagni, Giovanni Fattore, Andrea Fox, Carlos Urla Torres, Franca Masera, Elena Rebora, Patrizia Rebulla, Andrea Forti and Olivia Custer. We owe our thanks to all of you for asking us the right questions and for listening to us. With your help we have tried to make our ideas both easy to understand and to read.

We would also like to thank all the physicians, patients and students who have provided us with the examples we used in this book.

We also wish to thank CERGAS research centre librarian Chiara Peverelli, for her patience and invaluable assistance and the Bocconi University, Research Division, for providing us with a grant to work on this book.

Introduction

Communication theory affirms that a phenomenon must be viewed from a wide enough perspective in order to make sense of it. For example, an aging patient with chronic illness may face health challenges but may also be battling with loneliness and a sense of isolation. Patients' problems are broader than the scope of the organizations that treat them. Patients need professional relationships to cross the boundaries of departments and entire organizations in order to create a wide enough perspective to meet their needs.

Much of the management literature focuses on the hierarchy of the organization – how to manage subordinates, motivate employees and even manage the relationship with the boss – this book focuses on managing relationships between roles with equivalent organizational authority within and between healthcare organizations. This book introduces peer to peer relationships as an integral part of healthcare management.

Peer to peer relationship competence has been absent from both the literature and the change management field. Its absence is visible in the daily routine of managers at the very apex of the organization. The following two examples of a day in the life of a CEO in healthcare capture symptoms of peer to peer relationship dysfunction in the healthcare organization:

A CEO of a 600-bed hospital spent an hour listening to a patient's indignant relatives and another hour trying to understand how a rotten apple had made it through the hands of ten different employees and onto the dinner plate of the patient.

> A medical director of a 1,100-bed healthcare network asked herself how patients in critical condition were losing more weight due to mistakes in their meals than they were from their illnesses. The case in point was a week of crackers to a fragile oncology patient on a liquid diet.
>
> The crackers had been delivered to the patient's bed for seven straight days under the noses of many professionals on the floor, in the dietary department and in the kitchen.

Hierarchy is exasperated with managing what should be autonomous horizontal relationships in the healthcare organization. Like the many headed monster Hydra in Greek mythology, as soon as one rotten apple problem gets resolved, two more have grown in its place.

This book makes a case that horizontal integration between peers is a specific managerial competence. Peer relationships tend to be explained by members of the organization as either effective because friendly or ineffective because unfriendly. However, like being an effective manager has nothing to do with being friendly with subordinates, the relationship with peers is also a manageable quantity that is to be distinguished from personal likes and dislikes.

Peer to peer relationships follow patterns of dysfunction, and are not as arbitrary or as personal as they are often perceived. This book provides the conceptual frameworks for identifying these patterns and for developing effective horizontal competence necessary for managing the relationship with peers. Peer relationships can be made stronger by the organization and its culture. Lastly, management indicators, rational choice decision models and other managerial tools can be developed to increase the quality and effectiveness of peer to peer competence in the organization.

The examples described in this book come from healthcare organizations in the United States and in Italy. In these two countries both the cultural mores and the healthcare systems could not be more different: the United States has a private system and the Italian system is public. By illustrating examples of patterns of peer to peer integration in healthcare organizations across two cultures and systems, this book makes a case for the importance of peer to peer relationships in any healthcare organization in any culture. It is possible to manage these relationships and build these relationship skills.

Healthcare organizations depend more and more on managers who can create a broad enough perspective within and between departments and organizations to make sense of patient needs. When peer to peer relationships are well-managed, they produce appropriate and quality care at a sustainable cost to the healthcare organization.

The road map: a brief description of the chapters

This book is organized in six chapters. The first chapter identifies a gap between how organizational theory envisioned the concept of "role" and the degree to which people have personalized their roles in the organization. In organizational theory an organization can call itself such, if and only if, the people who work in it can be replaced at any time with other people with comparable credentials and skills. A role exists independently of the person in it. This guarantees the continuity and the replication of the organization itself. However, in reality, in healthcare management, many are the cases where the person is more important than the organization. In the United States, professionally talented and recognized physicians are not subject to the rules of the organization, as they are considered indispensable to organizational reputation. In Italy, these figures are literally referred to as the "barons" of healthcare as they personally create their own fiefdoms within the organization.

In reality then, a role is filled with a person in the healthcare organization, and this can lead to degrees of discretion in relationship management both within the organization and towards patients and colleagues inside and outside the organization. Peer to peer relationships are particularly subject to personal discretion. This chapter will analyse how "feeling relationships" substitute organization and how these work on the basis of personal likes and dislikes. This chapter introduces two frames for beginning to manage peer to peer relationships: a definition of role and a definition of peer to peer relationship effectiveness termed "the blended relationship".

The second chapter focuses on why peer to peer relationships are critical for delivering quality care to patients. The data on patient compliance reports that 50% of chronic patients across all ages and illnesses are non-compliant. Non-compliant patients are not letting their physicians manage their care, they are managing their own care. As patients suffer more and more from chronic disease, they turn to different physicians for aspects of their care. As the population ages, healthcare challenges are not only clinical but are also social: loneliness, depression and isolation are as integral to the health of the population as their physical well-being. Patients need multi-professional teams. They need the cardiologist to work with the neurologist and the oncologist and the social worker. Patients need professional relationships to cross the boundaries of departments and entire organizations. Without organized professional integration, the management function is no longer in the hands of the organization but moves into the hands of the patient. In addition, this chapter introduces examples of organization and management indicators that sustain peer to peer relationships in the healthcare organization.

The third chapter describes patterns of dysfunction in peer to peer relationships and therefore establishes that peer to peer dysfunction has nothing to do with personal likes or dislikes. John Nash's theory of the non-cooperative game and of equilibrium are used as the key to unravelling the dysfunctional patterns. This chapter sustains that peer to peer relationships systematically prefer non-cooperation and perceived relationship stability, over achieving optimal outcomes in the healthcare environment. On the other hand, examples of where relationship stability and optimal outcome were designed to be superimposed will show that multi-professional players can cooperate with one another and produce optimal outcomes even if they belong to different organizations. By analysing the characteristics of the non-cooperative game and the Nash Theory of Equilibrium, patterns of failure in horizontal relationships in healthcare management and how to manage those patterns will be discussed. The role of organization and negotiation theory as tools for bolstering self-enforced collaboration between peers are explored.

Chapter 4 is about what kind of organizational culture and language can favour the development of peer to peer relationships in the organization. Organizational and interpersonal trust are described as measures of performance and are presented as a more effective indicator of performance than customer satisfaction. Furthermore, as people generally do not trust someone or an organization just because they say they will do something, models of rational choice in decision making will be analysed as a language in which peers can discuss common problems. The theory of intuitive management and of non-verbal communication will be examined as examples of rational choice application in the healthcare organization.

Chapter 5 exemplifies how trust and rational choice in decision making work in the healthcare context. In this chapter the model is applied to research design and results. The research examines the quality of life of cancer patients undergoing chemotherapy. The research model suggests that trust and rational choice are excellent tools for peer to peer integration on the one hand and for better understanding the needs of patients on the other.

Chapter 6 identifies the horizontal relationship skill set that the healthcare manager needs to possess in order to be an effective manager. It translates diversity management and communication theory into a simple skill set that enables a manager to develop peer to peer blended relationships.

The conclusions of this book address the problem of acquiring these skills in the learning environment. This chapter addresses what a student should look for in a business school program, and how to use classroom interaction as a playground for building professional competence. Likewise, schools of management that offer health management programs which focus and diversify teaching methods can create a learning environment in which to practice and acquire these skills.

Kurt Lewin wrote "nothing is as practical as a good theory".[1] Therefore, this book hopes to make a contribution to the theory of management in healthcare by identifying systematic patterns in peer to peer relationships. The hope of the authors is that the theory of peer relationships has a practical value and therefore will also be helpful for the healthcare practitioner and for the student of management interested in working in healthcare.

1
The Peer to Peer Relationship: The Blended Relationship

Peer to peer relationships in healthcare organizations

As health problems get more complex and people live longer, people's health problems no longer fit neatly into the services provided by one division of the organization. An oncology patient can become diabetic. An obese patient can experience diabetes and heart disease. Problems of multi-dimensional chronic illness require services from different departments, even if the person experiencing these problems and receiving these services is one and the same.

The typical organizational structure is represented as a pyramid with an apex and a base. In every organization, managing relationships between peers, players with equal organizational authority, is complicated and when these relationships get steeped in conflict, the most obvious resolution can be found in the pyramid, in the hierarchical structure.

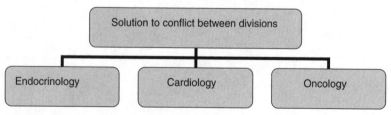

Figure 1.1   Hierarchy resolves conflict

In a military hospital in Italy, a one star general wrote an official reprimand to two physicians who both reported to him. They worked in different departments. It read:

"I order you two to get along better".

This is an amusing example of how hierarchy is exasperated with managing what should be autonomous horizontal relationships in the healthcare organization. It is emblematic of a larger problem.

> A CEO of an assisted living centre spent an entire morning with the relatives of a patient trying to unravel why a broken window shade still had not been repaired three weeks after they had reported it causing the patient to have to undress in plain sight of the neighbourhood.

Vertical management of horizontal relationships is simply inefficient, and in more strategic terms ineffective: it does not solve the real problem. Vertical management of peer to peer conflict drags down managers to work out problems in relationships way down the hierarchy.

Yet, every time the organization finds two or more critical players who are peers and who systematically do not get along, the solution tends to be to put a boss on top of them whose job it is to get them to collaborate or to compensate for the fact that they don't.

As this is a common problem, healthcare organizations suffer from becoming skyscrapers rather than pyramids. It is truly not unusual for "broken window shade" problems that could have been simply resolved between colleagues somewhere on the bottom of the pyramid to finish up at the apex of the organization weeks later.

In Italy an entire layer of hierarchy has been introduced with the role of Director of Department. Chief Medical Officers, exasperated with trying to negotiate and share strategies with Chief Physicians, were able to negotiate nationally, a level of hierarchy between the

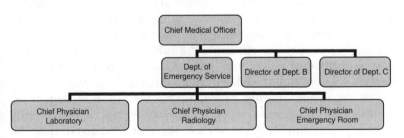

Figure 1.2   Adding layers to hierarchy

Chief Medical Officer and the Chief Physicians. These are known as Director of Departments and it is their job to make 3–4 Chief Physicians of interrelated departments work together as is depicted in Figure 1.2.

In Italy, the lack of peer to peer collaboration affected the quality and timeliness of responses: problems marched up the hierarchy without resolution. In the United States, on the other hand, reengineering became a popular tool for trying to respond more effectively. Reengineering said that value time (VT) divided by total time (TT) should tend to one $VT/TT=1$.[2] In the 21st century, proponents of reengineering argued, a demand for service should produce an immediate exhaustive response from the organization. If, for example, a patient's knee was hurting and it turned out he/she needed knee surgery, VT was all the time that the organization was actually doing something about the knee: diagnostic exams, surgery, rehabilitation. TT was the total time that was passing between when the patient expressed his/her need and when the patient was able to walk on the knee without pain.

Unfortunately VT/TT turned out to be .001 in the best organizations and .0001 in the average organization. Reengineering identified the need to radically reconsider organization.[3] Reengineering projects in the field eliminated middle management on the one hand, and proposed multi-tasking on the other. Together these were effective solutions to peer to peer relationships because they avoided them all together. Bluntly put, reengineering projects sustained that people whose job it was to watch people do the work, belonged to organizations that needed to be "right sized". This was a euphemism and it really meant fire the middle managers.[4]

But since middle managers existed so that people doing the work had someone to help them get along with one another, and since middle managers had been eliminated, roles needed to be reconfigured so that they did not need to get along with one another anymore. Roles were to become responsible for full service to clients and therefore no longer had to interact horizontally. Therefore, there was no need for a layer of hierarchy to order them, or cajole them or motivate them to get along. In healthcare services this full service concept applied to administrative roles but could not apply to clinicians. If a patient needed surgery, many players with equal weight were going to have to be part of the care process: surgeon, anaesthesiologist, radiologist, etc.

The purpose of these first paragraphs has been to show, with broad brush strokes, how healthcare organizations have sidestepped building peer to peer relationship competence. They have avoided it: either by managing these relationships with vertical authority or by redesigning roles so that they did not need to interact with peers.

Given that peer to peer relationships are so fundamental to organizational efficacy, it is hard to imagine how the healthcare organization could function without them. The fact of the matter is that peer to peer relationships exist in healthcare organizations, in a particular form. The rest of this chapter will discuss the relationship characteristics of the healthcare organization and what kind of peer to peer relationships we find in the healthcare organization today. The next paragraph discusses the differences between theory and practice in relationships in the healthcare organization.

Theory of relationships in the organization vs. practice

Organizational theory developed with the idea that an organization is characterized by the principle of continuity and replicability. The organization lives beyond those who work in it. This implies substitutability: no employee can be personally indispensable. Taylor first hypothesized this principle of organization in studying the industrial revolution. Taylorism, as Taylor's study of the organization became known, has permeated organizational theory, however the principle that remained throughout the development of organizations has been that an organization must work independently of the specific people in it.[5] This means that the organization is formed by a group of competencies that can be covered by a number of people with the necessary knowledge and experience, and can be substituted at any moment by another person with these credentials. The concept is that while people in the organization come and go, organizational roles, processes and procedures are created to sustain organizational survival over time.

The field of management emphasizes role design, organizational structure and processes. In fact, managing subordinates should have nothing to do with liking them. Management is a science, not a lottery. There are theories on how to motivate and encourage individuals and groups, regardless of specific personality compatibilities between the manager and the subordinate. Peer to peer relationships, or relationships between roles with equal organizational authority, on the contrary, have never been thought of as a science. When peer to peer relationships work, these are attributed to "feeling". When they don't work, people say to themselves "too bad, we don't get along", and they look for someone else to work with.

Today, in healthcare organizations and generally in public service organizations, the relationship among people in the organization has shaped how work gets done in a way that organizational theory did not anticipate. While organizational theory presumes substitutability, in many healthcare and public service organizations, relationships between people do indeed become indispensable. As every role is filled with a person, some organizations operate in a reality based on the relationships between people rather than the interaction between roles. While formal organizational charts, roles and procedures exist in these organizations, they do not reflect the way work gets done. These organizations are dominated by personal relationships rather than by organized exchanges between roles.

In the organization where personal relationships dominate, relationships with employees take place on a personal note rather than on the professional exchange of information connected to formal roles. This model is not necessarily a dysfunctional one and in many cases possesses all the characteristics of a centre of excellence. However, those centres of excellence built on personal relationships are difficult to replicate or transfer to other environments and have limited continuity. Reggio Emilia's nursery schools, for example, were cited by the Atlantic Monthly as the best pre-school system in the world; however, ten years later, this excellent system only characterizes the pre-schools in that province.[6] It had not been possible to replicate or transfer this experience to other regions of Italy because the relationships between the people working in the nursery schools determined the excellence of the organization. Healthcare organizations also may have departments that become centres of excellence, but the reputation of the centre of excellence finishes with the retirement or departure of certain members of the medical team. Therefore the personal relationship organization also suffers from discontinuity.

Anthropological study emphasizes the importance of relationships between people as the basis for groups, how they think, the rules that they give one another and the values they express. One way to examine relationships between people is to look at the role of the gift or an invitation in the relationship, a form and function of exchange. Mauss describes that to refuse a gift or an invitation is to refuse a relationship, and that there is a terribly thin thread between a festivity and a war. "To refuse to give, or to fail to invite, is – like refusing to accept – the equivalent of a declaration of war; it is a refusal of friendship and intercourse".[7] In the ancient Germanic languages "gift" had two meanings; "gift" and "poison".

On the other hand, to accept a gift is to establish a debt, and not returning an invitation or reciprocating a gift, is to accept a subordination. The tribe or group that forms on the basis of exchange can develop into a form of tribalism in which in-group loyalty among members who make exchanges is stronger than outside forces. The study of the healthcare organization and the relationships between people working in them finds many similarities to these observations: the relationships between people are a form of tribalism which is not responsive to organizational and managerial regulation, just as certain tribes do not fit in to the rules of the state. Professional groups in healthcare, for example MDs, nurses and technicians can be understood as groups with a greater in-group loyalty than acceptance of organizational regulatory mechanisms.

The next paragraph will explore how the personal nature of relationships within the organization can be observed by an outsider to the organization.

The organization inadvertently expresses its real nature to clients

All organizations inadvertently betray the true nature of their operating systems to their clients. The way relationships function inside the organization is reflected in how outsiders perceive the organization and its rules. Organizational image is a concept coined by Normann, to describe this reflection of the way things get done and states that "the image that the service company creates in the mind of its own staff and its environment will be largely determined by the nature of its service, its organization, its culture and its members...".[8] In defining image as a reflection of the organization, Normann implies that it is impossible to hide the nature of our relationships to third parties, who will understand them, and act accordingly. Image is generally used in the literature to denote a phenomenon of positive connotations, but image works like a mirror, reflecting what happens inside the organization. The image of internal culture and relationships is what is reflected to the user of the organization. This image will be called "inadvertent marketing" in this book because the image is often not communicated on purpose. The nature of the organization, its culture and members is inadvertently communicated to patients in the healthcare delivery organization.

Inadvertent marketing makes it possible to observe the organization where personal relationships dominate: anyone who has anything to do with the organization from clients to new employees, will understand that what one can get done depends on the person one deals with, and does not depend on organizational standards. Patients or citizens who insist on getting something they have identified as important will not take no for an answer. They have understood that in the organization anything is possible if you find the right person to help you. These considerations move the criteria for success from knowledge management to relationship management.

Personal relationships are not limited to vertical relationships or to managers with employees but also involve peer to peer relationships and relationships with clients of the organization. In many organizations feeling relationships develop between people for mysterious reasons. These often link people to one another across organizational divisions. These relationships may be born from a sympathetic chance encounter at the coffee machine, children who go to school together or other "personal feelings". Feeling relationships can be observed by watching phone manners in the organization. A feeling phone call always involves asking for a person by name. So the surgeon Dr. Brown will not phone Radiology and speak to whoever is on duty and answers the phone. He will phone Radiology and ask to speak with Dr. White. Whenever a peer activates a feeling relationship he/she will ask to speak to a specific person in order to obtain a service, general information, or a clarification.

Feeling relationships exist because people like one another, and override the organizational procedures because they are quick and because they create a hierarchy in fact in the relationship. When one person asks another for a favour, it is a way of giving an order, only it is invisible because it looks like a friendly thing to do. If a friend refuses a favour, the relationship moves from exchanging invitations to "war". So relationships can move from feeling to no feeling. Or relationships of no feeling may abound just as much as feeling ones do.

Feeling networks which are a chain of feeling relationships, involve certain people and not others. The same problem brought to Ms. Smith one day, and resolved immediately with five friendly phone calls, may take months if brought to Ms. Brown who does not belong to a similar feeling network, or chooses not to activate it.

In the public sector it is certainly not fair that for any given question there are two speeds with which the question can be answered. The feeling network is the network with a common sense solution and often bypasses the organization and the organizational competence of its roles. The formal organizational requirements are handled by the network ex-post so that nothing appears out of place. Feeling networks work around the organization, and find a solution quickly. They also leave the people in them with the idea that "organization is an obstacle to work around, not a tool to work with".

Many users of the National Health System do not take no for an answer and treat the organizational response as an "obstacle to work around". This is an effect of inadvertent marketing (it is impossible to hide the nature of our relationships).

In many healthcare services it is difficult to impose criteria such as "appropriateness" when the feeling relationships in organizations bypass organizational criteria. General practitioners (GPs) exemplify this problem with regards to appropriateness in pharmaceutical prescriptions. Patients choose their GPs and can change their choice at anytime. Consequently, GPs prefer to prescribe to an insistent patient rather than say no, even if the request is inappropriate, because they feel very sure that their patient will establish a feeling relationship with another GP who will say yes to the patient's request.

The following example of feeling relationships and how they work comes from the Emergency Room (ER) of one of the biggest public hospitals in Rome and a foundation in Rome, and is a concrete example of how feeling relationships are inadvertently communicated to users of services, betraying the fact that for the client, it is better to look for someone to help you, because the organization is an obstacle to work around.

Feeling relationships

One day, a Senegalese illegal immigrant limps into the ER and sits quietly on a chair in the waiting room. He is not admitted because he does not leave his name and a description of his symptoms with the triage nurse. The nurse on duty happens to see him walk in and notices that he has not stopped to register with the triage nurse. She is a traveller herself, and has often vacationed in Africa. She remembers what it was like to be sick and far from home. With all this in mind, she walks over to the Senegalese man and asks him what brings him to the ER. He explains, in perfect Italian: *"I am an illegal immigrant, I have this limp that keeps getting worse, I feel terrible pain when I put my weight on my leg, and it's becoming unbearable. I am afraid that if I do not get help, I will no longer be able to walk, and I do not know how I will survive"*.

The nurse takes his case to heart. Though his case is not an ER case (he is not in a life threatening situation) and his illegal immigrant status would require some bureaucratic procedures, she "bypasses" these obstacles and speaks directly to the physician on duty. She explains her feelings about travelling and feeling ill abroad, and she explains his case. The physician, with a familiar groan, says "show him in". The physician watches the Senegalese patient as he limps in the door and says to the nurse "he needs to see someone in orthopaedics". The nurse thinks a bit, remembers a person she knows who works in orthopaedics. She gives her a call and quickly confirms that the physician there is willing to receive him. The physician in orthopaedics looks at him as he limps painfully through the door and says "we need an x-ray". The ER nurse runs him down to the Radiology Division where she runs into the head technician whom she has

Feeling relationships – *continued*

known for years. She gives him the abbreviated version of the long and complicated story and the head technician has the x-ray done.

They go back up to the Orthopaedics Division. The physician takes the x-ray from the ER nurse and hangs it against the x-ray reader. He comments out loud "there is some cloudiness around the hip and in order to get a better impression I need a bone biopsy". The ER nurse is crestfallen, she has no way of procuring a biopsy for this man. She asks the physician if he would write on hospital stationery what the patient needs so that he doesn't waste time going through this process again. At this point she tells the Senegalese patient that there is a foundation that runs a private clinic for illegal immigrants under the central train station. She suggests that he take his x-ray and diagnostic needs to them to see what they can do.

He thanks her profusely and proceeds to the clinic. At the clinic the physician on duty receives the Senegalese patient who hands him the official hospital stationery from the Department of Orthopaedics with the word "biopsy". The physician smiles to himself and says "You have come to the wrong place, we are only equipped to offer a very basic response to problems of hygiene and health. We have no technical instruments whatsoever". Seeing that the Senegalese continues to look at him, he offers "I will show you around so that you know I am telling the truth". He takes him on a tour, and then says goodbye.

For five days straight, the Senegalese patient continues to return to the private clinic and speaks to a different physician every time. Word spreads about the Senegalese immigrant among the clinic's physicians because the request for a biopsy is so unusual. The doctor who first received him feels "undermined" – he says to his colleagues "I even showed him around, I don't understand why he didn't believe me".

Once again, the Senegalese patient returns, only to find the physician who had first received him. The physician is annoyed and concludes "I know you asked all my colleagues, but as you can see, I told you the truth the first time". The Senegalese patient continues to look at him.

"I don't see what I can do for you!!", exclaims the physician. He then gets an idea "you can speak with our Director, that way you will see that I have given you the full story". He marches the Senegalese into the Director's office and explains the whole story. The Director begins to answer as all the other physicians had: "We offer basic..." when he cuts himself off and asks "How long ago did you start limping?"

Looking for someone to help

In this case, the Senegalese patient has eight contacts with seven differ-ent physicians, and only at the very end of the story does he get asked: under which circumstances did this happen to you? This is a critical question, because this problem began just three weeks before. In fact, this patient had a sexually transmitted disease (STD) that caused pain in the abdominal region, and his problem had nothing to do with orthopaedics or with a "biopsy". The story ends happily ten days after the Director's question with an antibiotic treatment for the STD. However, the Senegalese patient learned early on, that it was not going to matter what the organizational rules said, it was going to matter that a person took a personal interest. That is why he did not take no for an answer while looking for a bone biopsy.

In this example, the ER nurse had friends in the Orthopaedics Division and in Radiology. These feeling relationships are one of the quickest orga-nizational response systems in existence. In the public sector, feeling rela-tionships offer faster results than any private sector organization.

Feeling relationships act independently of divisions and procedures within the organization. The nurse had many friends in the organization and was able to provide services and resolve problems as if she were the organization. In fact she assumed the role of boss in interacting with her peers because when she asked someone for a favour she was in fact man-aging their time and telling them what to do. When feeling is introduced into peer to peer relationships and feeling networks are formed, there is a "boss" of the network who is asking for favours and telling peers what to do next. In the case of the ER nurse, she asked various players for favours. Sharing information about the case itself on a professional level was not a concern of the members of the network. In this favour asking mode, she in fact established a hierarchy in the peer to peer relationship: she told the radiologist what to do. She even told the orthopaedic physician what to do. While from a formal perspective neither physician would allow a nurse to take control of their time and roles, in the feeling relationship these formal considerations are eclipsed by personal feeling. The role of the people in this story is compromised in a formal sense by the "feeling" between the people involved in the relationship. The excuse of feeling between people establishes a hierarchy between the person asking for favours (boss) and the person giving favours (subordinate).

If another illegal immigrant arrives when this nurse is on vacation, he may not even be asked what is wrong. Three issues arise. The first concerns inequity, the second quality, and the third appropriateness. When a citizen asks for services and falls into a feeling network the answer to a complex or an inappropriate question will be given in a miraculously short time. In this case we see that an illegal immigrant who did not have an emergency saw three doctors and got an x-ray even though he was not qualified to access these services. From a quality and appropriateness perspective, the services he received had nothing to do with his condition. It can be safely concluded that they were not cost effective services.

Furthermore, the breakdown of the formal organizational model is evident. A nurse had punched her time sheet in ER but was absent for over two hours. This creates more organizational dysfunction. Triage in the ER and waiting lists in various departments have been bypassed, which means that scheduled priorities and appointments will run late. Feeling relationships not only work around organization but indirectly weaken the pillars of organization.

While the speed of results in the feeling network is enviable, the quality of results is variable. As can be seen in this case, members of the feeling network were working for the network itself, and not for the patient. In the hospital, the patient saw two physicians three times, got x-rays and was told that he needed a biopsy, but at no time got asked what happened to him. This problem transfers to the new environment (the private clinic specialized in illegal immigrants).

This story exemplifies how inadvertent marketing works. The Senegalese man learns in one afternoon in the ER that "anything is possible if you find the right people to help you". He learns that the organization is an obstacle to work around.

Inadvertent marketing allows the user to see the true nature of the relationships and the culture of the organization.

Relationship map: identifying patterns of dysfunction[9]

The relationship map is a way of organizing and reading relationships in the organization. It provides a frame in which to place relationship management experience.

The "relationship map" describes the person's relationships. The feeling relationship where people like each other is expressed in the top left corner of the map. The no feeling relationship where people dislike one another is expressed in the lower right hand corner of the map. The map represents the person's relationships and tells us that people are sometimes helpful and sometimes not.

As can be observed in the "relationship map", two kinds of relationships seem to characterize interaction in the field today: feeling relationships and no feeling (bureaucratic) relationships. Feeling rela-

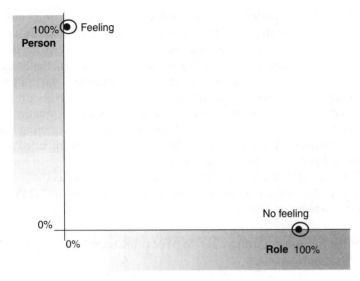

Figure 1.3   The relationship map

tionships take place between one person and another. They position
the person at 100% person and 0% professional role. They privilege the
person over the professional component of role, and see all forms of
organization as an obstacle around which to move. In an organization
that begins to work with a heavy influence of feeling relationships, we
see a "schizophrenic relationship map". The use of the term "schizophrenic" wishes to be evocative, and not clinical. What is observed is a
single person behaving in two diametrically opposed ways.

According to mood and feeling, the same employees will either
produce common sense results or retreat into a definition of role that is
so limited to what is formally requested as to appear that the role exists
but no human being is present inside that role (100% professional role,
0% person). Responses such as "Sorry I cannot help you, it is not my
department, I do not know who can help you", are examples of this. In
these cases, the internal or external client hits a wall in which it is not
possible to resolve the problem. Feeling and no feeling relationships do
not pertain to two separate groups of employees, but to the same
group. The no feeling position still uses organization as an obstacle. It
is used to repel someone else. Therefore, contrary to fantasies about
public service organizations which imagine a solid group of people
who never do anything, there are not two separate types of employees,
those that are dedicated to public service and those that are not. In
reality, the same person behaves differently in two different situations.

Chronically ill patients who access day hospitals many times during their care observe that their caretakers in the organization are available and friendly on some occasions and unavailable and unfriendly in others. In any case, from an anthropological perspective, patient care is a product of personal relationships and not of organizational design.

In organizations with these relationship characteristics, it is extremely difficult to introduce management tools: budget processes, quality processes, planning and control efforts. They are either worked around (seen as an obstacle) or become the opposite of what they were intended to be (used as a personal defence to say "NO").

The organizational map, with its two extremes, shows us that organizational theory did not describe what happened to relationships when people were put in them.

Frames for constructing peer to peer relationships into part of management science

Figure 1.4 illustrates that what may be missing in many organizations today is the concept of a blended relationship. The map below introduces the blended relationship as a model for building relationship competence over personal feeling-no feeling.

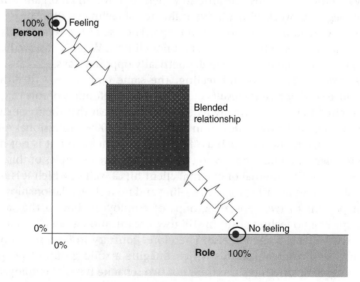

Figure 1.4   The blended relationship map

A blended relationship involves being a person inside the role you are asked to play in the organization. This new box in the "relationship map" is not a point on the map but an area. It is an area where people do not have to conform to rigid behavioural conduct, but do have to ground their relationships with their role. Organizations may not easily identify the need to construct blended relationships because feeling relationships are a smoke screen and make it difficult to see why it could be important. Certain conditions of change, like expansion, succession or crisis, may draw these organizations to include developing this blended relationship competence in their organizational culture.

Building blended relationship competence involves becoming a person within an organizational role. This is another way to guarantee "patient care". Blended relationships place the "care" function in the team and respect professional competence rather than relying exclusively on the personal relationship.

The concept of a person in a role is complex, however, the story of the Senegalese patient demonstrates that the nurse acted on "personal discretion". A person in a blended relationship would act on professional discretion rather than on personal discretion. The following is a true story, emblematic of how blended relationships apply to physician patient relationships too. This next example was told by the chief physician of a laboratory in a busy urban hospital:

> I worked for years on the basis of organizational theory to make the laboratory efficient. However I was overwhelmed by the degree to which everyone used the emergency room to get things done in a hurry. As I became more and more discouraged I took to hiding from the public. The waiting room space was inadequate and the patients filled all the sitting space and then all the standing room in the corridor. One day I was summoned by the CEO to discuss my budget, and I emerged into the corridor full of people waiting. A woman blocked my path and with beautiful manners asked me "could I steal a minute of your time?" I looked around nervously, this is exactly the reason I try to avoid contact with the waiting public. But her manner was so polite, that I made myself available.
>
> This is what she told me: she had been diagnosed with a tumor by her oncologist and had to do blood exams to establish the chemotherapy treatment. As she put it: "I feel I can overcome my illness by acting as quickly as possible, not letting any time go by waiting, this really means something to me, it makes me feel like I am helping myself to

get better". I thought of all the people waiting who may have had the same diagnosis. I decided that many people may need time to absorb the shock of such a diagnosis. I made an exception. I bypassed the official system and her exams were done in half an hour.

She thanked me profusely. Several months later I received a phone call from the same woman. I was about to say "what can I do to help you" but I stopped myself and waited to hear what she had to say. These were her words: *"I will be coming to the hospital for the last time today. Unfortunately, my cancer has progressed and I am terminally ill. I called to thank you, what you did for me allowed me to live this part of my life as the active person that I am"*.

The chief physician concluded: "If I came across this situation again, I would do what I did again, even though it had no clinical effect on the progression of the disease".

The issue of professional discretion in fact revolves around two issues. The first is, "if it happened again, would I do it again?" This is one of the factors that distinguishes professional discretion from personal discretion. The other is that the discretion that occurs is in the organizational territory of the person who exercises it. Unlike the ER nurse who directs the patient to areas where she has no technical competence, the chief physician in this story bends the rules of his own professional domain, not someone else's. In so doing he assumes professional risk in his own field.

In the service organization, the blended relationship puts a person in every role, so to speak. This applies not only to those working in the organization but also to those seeking an organizational response. The woman who asked for exams "right away" expressed how her person interpreted the role of patient. The patient herself showed professional discretion, she formulated her need, which may or may not belong to others in her situation, to act quickly. Both acted in a constructive blended relationship. The third position represented on the relationship map, the blended relationship, is hard to find in today's organization but represents an opportunity for managers trying to create a higher quality and appropriateness of response to patient needs.

A model for building blended relationship competence

Roles in organization have many different definitions. However, a practical understanding of a blended relationship is composed of three parts: technical competence, relationship management, and reciprocal expectations.[10]

Technical competence is the competence which the organization is seeking and can be met with work experience, practical experience or education. Some examples might include a computer programmer who may or may not have education or work experience, a medical degree for the physician role, etc... Technical competence is generally an attribute that the person possesses independently of the organization.

Relationship management has to do with connecting the technical side of one's role to outside influences, organizational goals, and the technical competence of others in the organization. Relationship management asks the person with technical competence to apply professional knowledge to the resources available to the organization and to come up with a solution that will function in this organization.

Reciprocal expectations has to do with "expecting to be consulted" about a matter that involves the technical competence. While people are very sensitive and react strongly to their own expectations, they inadvertently tend to disregard the expectations of others. The most compromised facet of the role is apparently the "technical competence" but in reality, it is the "expectation". The following example illustrates insensitivity towards the expectations of other peers.

The bowles court

In a small town of 7,000 inhabitants and 40 employees, the City Council met and decided to promote a bowles court.

The municipality held a meeting known as the Management Conference after every political session. Political objectives were defined on Wednesday nights at the City Council, and the "conference of management" took place on Friday mornings at the Town Hall. The structure of a local authority defines the political arena as the place where goals are set, and the municipality as the place where it is decided how to realize these goals.

The person who coordinated the conference of management was the Secretary General. He attended the political session and passed information to the organization.

The Secretary General had prepared a perfect meeting. Each participant had been given an agenda for the morning meeting. The table was set up in a horseshoe so that everyone could see everyone else. The meeting began on time. Each participant had a bottle of water. The Secretary took notes on the white paper board.

The Secretary General began the meeting by describing the objective that had been agreed upon in the City Council: a bowles court. The Bowles Players Association of the town had made a formal

The bowles court – *continued*

request to the mayor for a bowles court, as they had formed an association but had nowhere to play. The mayor had accepted their request with enthusiasm and had promised that he would give an answer as to how, where and when the court would be built.

The Technical Manager opened an architects' draft sheet and showed "the project". The project was technically beautiful. In the town, there was an old liberty style greenhouse that had collapsed. It was a metal structure with hundreds of little glass windows. The Technical Manager made the following proposal: restructure the greenhouse, place an Olympic size bowles court inside (Olympic because that way the neighbouring towns would be envious), total cost of the operation would be 150,000 Euros.

Needless to say, for a town of 7,000 inhabitants this was an extraordinarily expensive proposal for a bowles court. There was a long silence in the room.

Finally, the Police Chief (who always was dressed in uniform, and insisted on being called "chief" even though he was chief of one policewoman and there was one traffic light in the town), spoke up. He said: *"Your project is very beautiful. I just wanted to make a contribution. I have a different area of work. I work for the safety of the town's streets and so I see what happens here everyday. Every morning the retired men from the town and the outskirts appear in the early morning at the Bar Sport. Each one brings a newspaper, either about sports or news. About 30 of them are there by 8.15 in the morning and they create big groups and have animated debates about sports, politics or today's young people. At exactly 1pm they go back home to eat lunch. When they come back in the afternoon they no longer aggregate at the bar. They wander around and look lonely. I find one on a bench, one looking at a shop window, one strolling by himself, and so on. So my intuition is that the request for a bowles court comes from this group, they are looking for something to do together in the afternoon. So I don't see why we don't simply hire a tractor, make an outdoor bowles court in the town's public park, buy the bowles balls and leave them at the Bar Sport. If it rains, they won't be able to play, but it will take us less than a week, and well, let me think, no more than 100 Euros to fulfil their request.*

How did the two actors, the Technical Manager and the Police Chief, see their roles? In this case, the Technical Manager saw his role as exclusively the expression of technical competence. So much so that he had no expectation that the Management Conference would be useful in preparing the project itself. He had come to the encounter with a solution that the others were meant to accept, not to discuss. In fact, judging from his behaviour, in his view, the meeting was an unnecessary obstacle. The concept of blended peer to peer relationships in management is missing in this figure's understanding of role.

The Police Chief showed that he had a higher expectation of the meeting. He brought his technical expertise, and put it to work for the declared objective of the meeting: the bowles court.

This little case demonstrates that a shared definition of blended relationship was not present in the organization. In this state of affairs, the Management Conference does not assume value for its members: ironically it was an obstacle to the organizational objective and was seen as "a professional obstacle" by its members.

So far, the story confirms that a role is technical competence (architectural in the case of the Technical Manager, security in the case of the Police Chief).

Exercising a role is about the ability to put technical competence into a relationship with the organizational objectives and with the others in the organization (the Police Chief draws the conclusion that the association for bowles players are the retired men looking for something to do together in the afternoon).

But that is not all. The role is also, as previously illustrated, a reciprocal expectation, and this will be explored in the last part of the story.

Recognizing symptoms of relationship conflict in the organization

At this point the Technical Manager rolled his chair away from the table, his arms were crossed, and his face had changed colours several times; he had not spoken, but his "non-verbal" communication expressed his anger.

The Manager of Social Services stood up (everyone else was seated). She declared: "The elderly population is mine".

This was followed by a contagion of affirmations on behalf of all members of the conference as to who was responsible for what. The Finance Director stated "I was asked to make a budget at the beginning of the year (which by the way, nobody helped me with), the purpose of the budget was to plan the activities of the year. Was there mention of the bowles court? No. There was not. Therefore, it is absolutely indifferent to me whether it costs 100 Euros or

---

Recognizing symptoms of relationship conflict in the organization – *continued*

150,000 Euros to make a bowles court, in either case I refuse to modify the budgeted activities". All participants continued along these lines.

The Secretary General stole a glance at his watch, the time had run out for the meeting. He looked up and said, "Time is up, I feel comfortable closing this meeting with the following conclusion: lit is not possible to construct a bowles court in this town".

This last part of the story paints a portrait of the peer to peer relationships in the Management Conference. The discussion of this case will demonstrate that peer to peer relationships actually suffer from systematic problems even though they appear to suffer again and again from no feeling between two individuals.

Blended peer to peer relationships, as demonstrated in this last episode, require an attention to "expectations"; one's own and those of others. This is demonstrated, though negatively, by the behaviour of the Police Chief who suggests a solution to the Technical Manager's problem.

This case demonstrates that the actors in the organization had little understanding of blended peer to peer relationships in the organization. While it would appear that the Technical Manager and the Chief of Police do not like each other's style, in fact their conflict is structural and has nothing to do with their specific personalities.

Each role in an organization has a technical competence that in fact represents "organizational territory". In this example, the Technical Manager was reacting to something that could be described as "invasion of his organizational territory". The anger he expressed had to do with the impertinence of the Police Chief who was doing "his job" suggesting a tractor, the costs and the results of an alternative project. He felt his "role territory" had been invaded in front of the entire management group. If peer to peer roles interact in a formal organizational setting without respecting "organizational territory" they do not respect the "expectation" of role.

The "defence of organizational territory" happens when a peer suggests a solution to another peer. The rage this generates in the Technical Manager is systematic to all peer to peer relationships. So much so, that other peers in the group, even though they were not involved personally, reacted as if they were. In this case, the behaviour of the Police Chief incensed the Manager of Social Services who affirmed that the elderly population was hers. The Director of Finance also felt incensed, with people making investments that had not been budgeted.

This exemplification shows that while a peer can add perspective to a problem (I think the bowles association represents the retired men in the town), if the peer solves a problem for someone else (so this is what you should do), the peer to peer relationship collapses. This conflict is systematic, and will reoccur. It is not personal.

The defence of organizational territory creates a new objective for the group and displaces the organizational one. The new objective is to establish "who does what here". The bowles court had become a menace to organizational territory and in fact is completely eliminated from the discussion. In the future, the bowles court will probably become known simply as "a sensitive issue" because it will remind people of organizational chaos and instability. What appears to be a conflict between "subjects" would actually repeat itself even if the people around the table were switched with new people.

The Secretary General is faced with two possible ways of building a bowles court but decides that neither will work. In fact he is treating the bowles court as a "sensitive issue". This is because in many cases forcing a decision and ignoring the defensive positions assumed in the peer to peer relationship goes nowhere fast. The public administration is full of decisions that finish in an area known as "obstructionism". Realizing either one of the two proposals that emerged during the Management Conference would create an official winner and loser of organizational territory. A peer who has been attacked by another peer will do everything in his or her realm of possibility to avoid losing organizational territory. So a decision imposed by the hierarchy on two peers in a territorial conflict will be extremely costly and probably not produce the bowles court in the long run. The Secretary General opted for a "*status quo ante*" rather than force a decision. He avoided the risk of feeding a turf war.

If we assume that a role is group of competencies, technical, relationship and expectations, the role of the manager is to facilitate the integration of different technical competencies inside the box of blended relationships. The current practice in selecting CEOs is indicative of what is really expected of today's manager. Often we see a CEO of one company (for example, industrial), move and become a CEO in a new area of business (such as telecommunications).

The idea is if management is about facilitating technical competence already present in the organization, then it does not matter if the CEO is a technical competent himself. The Peter Principle says "everyone reaches their level of incompetence".[11] Obviously, those at the pinnacle of the organizational hierarchy have by definition reached their level of incompetence. The theory of management, that allows for a top manager to not possess technical competence of any relevance, takes for granted that the apex of the organization is technically incompetent. Healthcare sector CEO positions in Italy have recently been assigned to individuals with CEO experience in the private sector but with no previous experience in healthcare.

If the concept of role as a group of competencies, technical, relationship and expectations, is in fact possessed only by the manager, it would be extremely difficult to manage an industry that is outside "one's area of experience". Every member of the organization needs to understand what a role is and that it is represented in three dimensions: competence, relationships and expectations. A blended relationship is a relationship in which both actors are working in three role dimensions: competence, relationship management, and recognizing mutual expectations.

If members of the organization do not understand what a role is, then the manager must seek to stop peers from being rude to one another, and angering one another. The manager has to educate a role not to furnish a-specific common sense solutions to a peer with expertise in the field at hand. This is a difficult if not impossible task: take the example of the Police Chief. Who knew he was about to invade the Technical Manager's territory by suggesting that the organization rent a tractor? It takes a very careful manager to see where the Police Chief is going with his comment. An ideal manager would put a stop after the description of "afternoon loneliness", turn to the Manager of Social Services and ask for that expert opinion, then to the Finance Director for the financial issues. Few managers are able to "read the future" with this level of expertise.

This means that understanding how to create blended relationships in the organization is a competence that needs to belong to all figures in the organization. The manager can still be responsible for relationships and expectations but only after each member of the organization begins to work within the framework of assuming an organizational role: recognizing technical competence, relationship management and reciprocal expectations.

Recent developments in criminology have studied a theory called the "Collective Efficacy". This theory contests the idea that criminals grow out of poor, uneducated and racially diverse neighbourhoods. In the study of these situations it was found to be true in some cases while utterly false in others. So what made for "criminal behaviour"? Criminologists discovered that in some neighbourhoods, members of the community assumed an active role in the management of the community, while in other less successful communities, members were passive. Specifically the differences were visible; in one neighbourhood was a community garden and in the other, an empty lot full of drug dealers. The behaviours that differentiated one from the other were the collective assumption of blended roles. Everyone in the community was in a relationship with other community members and exercised a role in three dimensions.[12]

This metaphor is useful for public healthcare organizations. A CEO void of technical competence cannot be expected to work effectively in organizations where no one activates blended relationships. The CEO can decide either to dedicate technical competence to the issues at hand (not generally effective) or to build the sense of community (hard but not impossible).

Public sector management is particularly delicate as "feeling-no feeling" relationships and "feeling solutions" abound among peers and efficiency is often characterized by actions taken outside of the organizational frame and outside the box of peer to peer blended relationships. The peer to peer blended competence is an indispensable tool for horizontal integration. As local hospitals and local health authorities merge and become responsible for a large population and number of employees, these relationships become a critical tool for constructing effective peer to peer integration in a moment of "organizational growth". This is also true in smaller "centres of excellence" as they position themselves for the future, or for the "organizational succession of the leader".

Blended relationships: technical competence, relationships and reciprocal expectations, can be seen as a particularly useful tool in constructing peer to peer integration in large and complex organizations. Peer to peer integration is necessary in order to produce patient care as an attribute of the organization rather than as an attribute of the personal relationship.

As quality of life and managing chronic and degenerative illness become an important issue in patient care, blended relationships are the organizational background for constructing positive outcomes with patients. These blended relationships need to respond to the "subjective" expectation of the patient.

Problems in healthcare concerning patient compliance with treatment indicate that just as members of the organization do not assume their roles, often patients do not assume their roles either. The principle of inadvertent marketing is at work: the healthcare professionals are inadvertently showing patients how to get out of their roles. Patients who do not comply with treatment and therefore do not work for their own health are an example of how roles can be an extremely important management tool in the healthcare arena. This makes managing patient relationships a particularly difficult realm of management in healthcare today.

The following chapter applies the concept of blended relationship competence and professional discretion to the relationship between physician and patient. Furthermore, it explores the importance of organization in sustaining the blended relationship model.

2
Managing the Relationship with Patients

Introduction: the physician-patient relationship and healthcare management

"Illness is the night-side of life, a more onerous citizenship. Everyone who is born holds dual citizenship, in the kingdom of the well and in the kingdom of the sick. Although we all prefer to use only the good passport, sooner or later each of us is obliged, at least for a spell, to identify ourselves as citizens of that other place".[13]

Healthcare systems are designed to deliver healthcare services to citizens of that "other place" and to consume limited resources in an appropriate manner, balancing the good of the greater society with the needs of the single patient.[14] There are many indicators that the real managers of these resources are not the health systems themselves but the patients and their families. The following paragraphs will explore how this happens and why the doctor-patient relationship is critical in the "assumption" of management roles on the part of patients and their families. How to bring management back into the health system will be explored using the blended relationship model described in the previous chapter.

The purpose of this chapter is to reread the doctor-patient relationship as a product of the organizational context rather than a problem of interpersonal communication. The person, the individual with a specific character and personality, in the blended relationship model discussed in the previous chapter, has significant implications in managing physicians as well as patients. The examples in the previous chapter show how the blended relationship model adapts management tools to the needs of the people in the roles: there is no one best solution, but there is a way to read the problem. The complexity of healthcare management does not lie in producing huge quantities of information, but the key information for facilitating the blended relationship at hand. The outcome of patient care, that is, patient compliance, is a particularly important indicator of effective health system management.

Management in the hands of the patient

Assumed power, according to French and Raven,[15] is the power that people acquire by taking it without being specifically authorized to do so, and no one stops them. A terrorist who takes hostages, for example, has assumed power. There are many driving factors which bring the patient to manage healthcare resources. These include literacy of the patient, compliance, hypochondria, and malpractice. These will be explored below.

Medical care has grown dramatically in complexity for the patient. Just one example might be a patient with congestive heart failure. In the past these patients were prescribed two medications, digoxin and diuretics. "Today they are asked to take up to five different medications and to undertake a series of complex and repetitive self-care tasks: weighing themselves daily, reporting weight changes to their physician, controlling sodium and fat in their diets, etc..."[16] Physicians themselves worry about the increased complexity in the content of the messages that get passed to patients. This complexity affects patients in almost every area of medicine, from diabetes to asthma.

This obviously becomes even more critical if the patient has any kind of trouble understanding what is to be done. Illiteracy is a very big problem and the results of the *National Adult Literacy Survey* in the United States indicate that 22% of the population cannot find a street on a map, find two pieces of information in a sports article or fill out a form asking for their background information. Another 27.5% of the population cannot write a brief letter explaining an error on a bill or identify information from a bar graph.[17] These two populations, the first "functionally illiterate" and the second, "marginally illiterate", account for nearly half of the population in the United States and these literacy impediments create a great barrier to understanding basic health information. For example, 26% of patients at two public hospitals did not understand when their next appointment was and 42% could not understand what it meant to take "medication on an empty stomach".[18] This is a particularly difficult issue to overcome because people with limited literacy tend to hide their difficulties, even from their families. In a study in which patients were asked to declare whom they never told about these problems, 85% hid the situation from coworkers, 75% from healthcare providers, 68% from their spouses, and 52% from their children.[19] The social shame connected to illiteracy is enormous and studies report that patients hide their illiterate condition from their physician with phrases like: "I forgot my glasses today".

Immigrants share the difficulties of the functionally and marginally illiterate and have cultural reference points that may add to the communication problems described above. Gender roles, beliefs concerning blood, magic medicine and discomfort in answering direct questions are all among the specific problems in managing the health of immigrants.

The consequences of these problems on resource utilization in the health system is evident: missed appointments, emergency room visits and worsening health conditions. The patient manages the health system. The economic consequences of limited literacy are estimated at US $50–73 billion per year.

While literacy and immigration may be determinants of non-compliance in patients, they are not the only driving factors. Longer life spans and early diagnosis have created a significant population with chronic disease. While there are good clinical response systems to contain these diseases and manage them at the early stages, patients who do not feel sick have been unresponsive to making lifestyle changes that would be necessary to keep disease at bay. The progression of the disease, regardless of its early identification, has been an indication that compliance is low. For example, the more "silent" the symptoms of the disease are, as in the case of hypertension, the less the patient perceives a need to comply. The effects of mild to moderate hypertension on quality of life are described as "none".[20] The problems of compliance, when measured, are enormous. In a study of elderly patients with congestive heart failure, 90% of the population did not fill enough prescriptions to have daily congestive heart failure medication for the entire year and on average did not take medication on 111 days out of 365.[21]

In general, non-compliance across all age groups in long term treatment regimens has been estimated to be about 50%.[22] This means that 50% of patients in long term treatment are the managers of their own care.

Hypochondria is another cost to the health system of any country. Hypochondria is described as the "chronic preoccupation with the idea of having a serious disease. The preoccupation is usually poorly amenable to reassurance".[23] In the United States, it is estimated that 6% of patients visiting a general practitioner are hypochondriacs and it is estimated that the "unnecessary visits and examinations" they undergo costs the US health system US $20 billion in "wasted" resources.[24, 25] While the clinical focus of hypochondria has been on behavioural therapy for the patient and anti-depressants, there are important implications for the doctor-patient relationship. Studies have shown that physicians should establish a fixed number of visits, never accept emergency visits from these patients, work in a medical team (not individually) with these patients and use their authority as physicians during the patient's visit.[26] Therefore, the communication between physicians, which represents the organizational response to building the relationship with the patient is a vital tool to diminish these "wasted resources".

The statistics are overwhelming, but the problems are not limited to these macro-areas. Patients and their families are equally prone to assuming power. Malpractice litigation costs hospitals and physicians in the United States US $97.5 billion a year.[27] "According to recent studies, the reason people sue doctors and healthcare organizations is insensitive communication after a clinical incident".[28] In fact, 75% of malpractice suits are caused by the physician's communication style and attitude.[29] In particular the following items have supported this data: the explanation of the diagnosis, the explanation of treatment, the patient felt ignored, the physician did not consider the concerns of patients or relatives, the physician did not take into consideration their values, and the patient felt rushed.[30, 31]

Where the physician-patient relationship has gone astray: communication theory

Communication theory sheds some light in identifying the principal characteristics of the physician-patient relationship. In communication theory, the doctor-patient relationship is called a complementary relationship. This is a relationship based on the difference in which each player in the relationship occupies a position: in the case of a doctor-patient relationship the physician occupies a "one up" or primary position, and the patient occupies a "one down" or secondary position. The primary and secondary positions are not value judgements (strong-weak, good-bad) but objective observations of the dynamic of the relationship. Other examples might be teacher-student, mother-child, manager-employee. The relationship is like the two wheels that are interlocking, however it emphasizes difference.[32]

The physician-patient relationship is a unique form of complementary relationship in the service industry. Most front office contacts in the service industry are staffed by competent employees, who handle customers from all walks of life. The post office, an airline check-in counter, a certification office in a municipality are all examples of direct contact between the organization and the customer. However, these service employees are relatively anonymous in their professional world, they do not possess years of education and on-the-job training. In the university setting, professors are managing relationships with students who are pursuing a higher education, and so the cultural divide between professors and students is existent but not overwhelming. In the physician-patient relationship, a professor of surgery, renowned in the world, and not only his/her country, may be in a relationship with a patient who has no formal education. The complementary relationship is, in this case, particularly different.

Communication theory introduces an important aspect of human communication, known as "meta communication", however, to try to make it easier to understand, this will be termed "proposed relationship". Every human communication contains a "content" and a "proposed relationship". The content of the communication concerns the topic that the communication is addressing. In a physician-patient relationship, an example of the content of the relationship could be a back and forth on the health status of the patient.

The proposed relationship of the communication is the part in which the people communicating establish or fail to establish the nature of their relationship. This proposed relationship may be complementary or symmetrical. In the physician-patient relationship the complementary nature of the relationship is visually represented with many props and non-verbal signals: the physician wears the white coat while the patient wears the pyjama, the physician stands by the bed while the patient lies in it.

As this example demonstrates, proposed relationships can be non-verbal and represented in how people are dressed and in the décor of the setting. Office size, number of windows and the presence of a personal secretary are all signals as to the proposed relationship in the communication. In an office, a big chair behind the desk, and a smaller chair in front of the desk uses the furniture to describe the complementary proposed relationship.

In the office of important people, there are generally two possible settings for communication. One setting consists of a big fancy chair behind the desk and a smaller chair in front of the desk. The other, in another part of the same office, is a round meeting table with chairs that are all the same size. The proposed relationship will change according to which of the two settings is chosen for communication. Proposed relationships are called proposed, because they may not always be accepted by both parties.

To sum up with an example, the simple affirmation: "open the window immediately" shows us content and proposed relationship. The content of the message is "window" and the window may be open or closed. The proposed relationship in the message establishes the nature of the relationship between the two actors in the communication. In this example, the proposed relationship dictates: "I decide, you execute" and this may be accepted or rejected. If it is rejected, one possible response might look like "you open the window". The content of the message is an area of agreement, but the proposed relationship is not. The following table represents the possible combinations of content and proposed relationship in human communication:

Table 2.1 Content and proposed relationship

Content	Proposed Relationship
Yes	Yes
No	No

There are four possible combinations of response in any human relationship. The doctor-patient relationship is an excellent example of how content and proposed relationship may mix:

Yes to content and **Yes** to proposed relationship: This is a case of compliance. The doctor makes a diagnosis and instructs the patient, who in turn follows instructions. The analysis furnished above indicates that this outcome occurs about half the time, and sometimes as little as 10% of the time.

Yes to content and **No** to proposed relationship: This situation is one in which the physician is rejected by the patient; "doctor-shopping" often occurs as a consequence. Doctor-shopping means the patient turns to one physician after another, despite the fact that the physicians concur on the diagnosis and treatment. The patient will stop doctor-shopping when the proposed relationship is satisfactory.

No to content and **Yes** to proposed relationship: This situation is one in which the physician is accepted by the patient, but the care model proposed is rejected. This can be an area of negotiation between the physician and the patient but in many cases, simply causes a great sense of "impotency" in the physician. One example is described by a general practitioner:

> Elisa was the daughter of a very Catholic family. I was their family doctor, and so over the years came to know all members of the family very well. Elisa married and she and her husband desired above all else, to have children. Shortly after their marriage, Elisa got pregnant. I suggested that as part of the pre-natal screening process, she undergo amniocentesis. She refused. She told me that even in the event of pathology, her religious beliefs would not allow her to contemplate abortion. Her first child was born, unfortunately with terrible malformations, suffered immensely, and died at five months. Elisa was devastated. I suggested that she and her husband undergo compatibility tests to understand whether the health problems with their first child were of a genetic origin. They did these and the results were discomforting. I highly advised the couple to adopt a child, as did the specialists who did the tests. A few months later Elisa was pregnant again. She refused to do any tests to get information on the health status of the child. Her second child was a healthy boy. Again, I strongly discouraged attempting to have other children, now that they had been lucky and had one of their own, and I again suggested adoption. Shortly after the birth of her second child, Elisa was pregnant again. After her second child, she gave birth to six children all of whom died within the first six months of their lives. All died with tremendous suffering. I felt helpless as a physician and frustrated with Elisa. She kept coming back to me, but she never once took my advice.

No to content and No to proposed relationship: This is a situation of disconfirmation. The patient not only does not recognize the content of the message but denies the existence of the physician. The following example represents the difficulty of this situation:

> *"A man in his mid-60s had lung cancer and was facing death. He had from the start been negative and in a state of denial about his illness. There had been no indication that he wanted to acknowledge or talk about the fact that he would never recover. Everyday he waited for 'a miracle'. He begged the doctor to try everything possible, even when there were no more additional treatments which would influence or slow the progression of the disease. When the doctors refused to give him any 'hope' of recovery, he sought out one alternative treatment after another. His wife and two children experienced growing despair. They realized that he would die... They asked me repeatedly for help in talking to him about their grief. They wished to say goodbye in a dignified manner.*

> *... This man was a company manager, with responsibility for several hundred employees. For the last three to four years, he had shown great strength and enthusiasm in building up his business... His eldest child had been killed in a traffic accident. He had dealt with this situation by burying himself in this work. No one had seen him cry following the accident. His solution to the situation was to work longer hours and avoid talking about his child...*
>
> *I made several unsuccessful attempts to make the man open up emotionally and help him see that 'the battle was lost'. His refusal lead me to make a last attempt. I took his latest x-ray pictures with me, determined to show them to him even if he did not want to see them. With his children and wife present, I explained the x-rays to him, which show extensive spreading of his lung cancer. The desired result failed to materialize. He turned his face towards the wall, pulled his quilt over his head and asked us to leave the room. He died ten days later in abject loneliness."*[33]

The doctor-patient relationship has traditionally followed a disease-centred model. The disease-centred model focuses on the physician acquiring selected information for an accurate diagnosis. The doctor uses the relationship with the patient to ask questions which direct the differential diagnosis in the decision trees of the doctor. The typical disease-centred relationship sees the doctor asking questions and interrupting the patient if the patient digresses from the doctor's areas of exploration. Therefore in simple terms, the doctor uses the patient to focus the diagnosis which is usually then confirmed with medical tests. Following the diagnosis the physician prescribes medication and other forms of care to the patient. The definition of the word prescribe is "to write at the beginning, dictate, order or specify with authority"[34] – or, as in the case described above, explain that there is nothing left to be done. The prescription represents the relationship between doctor and patient. This relationship has dominated Western medicine for years. It has also produced significant improvements in the health of the patients. It establishes the doctor as the "manager" of the patient, and the patient as the "executor" of the doctor's orders.

Beyond the physician-patient relationship: the role of inadvertent marketing

As described in the previous chapter, inadvertent marketing suggests that it is only possible to "externally market" what is true inside the organization. If the organization wants to offer flexible services to clients, personnel inside the organization have to have a degree of autonomy concerning rules and procedures. One example to illustrate this concept was given by Sabena Airlines. Externally, Sabena advertised it took special care of business travellers. A businessman arrives at check-in and realizes that he has left his passport and ticket at the hotel where he was staying. The check-in counter calls the hotel and pays for the taxi to deliver the documents. No authorizations are necessary. The role of the check-in counter personnel is designed to meet client's needs. This illustrates that what can be sold outside as service has to be designed inside. Conversely, what happens outside (to customers) can be understood by looking at the dynamic inside the organization. Just as designing for service requires external marketing to match internal organization, the inverse function, what happens outside can be explained by what happens inside the organization. This inverse function was called "inadvertent" marketing in the first chapter. This translates into "the nature of our relationships with customers are imprinted by the relationships within the organization, it is impossible to hide these from our customers".

The disease-centred model characterizes the physician-patient relationship. Therefore, through inadvertent marketing, the disease-centred model must characterize the relationship within the organization, between professionals. Indeed, the disease-centred model is the model of communication in which doctors learn. When senior physicians make the rounds of the ward with younger and less experienced physicians they stop at the patient's bedside and point out what a disease looks like. Groopman provides an example of the relationship between physicians and physicians and that between physicians and patients in the formative stages of his medical training:

> "'It's a really great case' the neurology resident said. 'Gerstmann's syndrome'. I was a third year medical student, and neurology was my first clinical rotation. The resident listed the four findings associated with the disorder: agraphia, right-left disorientation, finger agnosia and acalculia. 'Due to a tumor in the parietal lobe' he explained.
>
> *We entered the patient's room. A dishevelled man in a hospital gown looked at us uncertainly. The resident had the man attempt a series of tasks and manuevers demonstrating all the elements of the syndrome's tetrad.*"[35]

David Biro, a dermatologist who is diagnosed with a rare form of leukaemia, in a personal account of his illness, had occasion to reflect on patient care both as a physician and as a patient.[36] While practicing dermatology, he recalls the medical culture, which attributes the highest value to cases that no one has seen before. He describes how, in dermatology, physicians would get excited over what they termed a "zebra". A "zebra" was a rare skin disease. The physician recounts that when he found his first zebra, a patient his age with a never before documented skin disease, he felt excited. He wanted to tell his colleagues, he wanted to write a paper. In general, in hospitals, patients are used to exemplify symptoms, so that physicians can learn the patterns of the disease. The zebra culture within the healthcare organization passes the disease-centred doctor-patient relationship from chief physicians to interns, and the communication patterns within the organization continue to encourage the disease-centred relationship with the patient. In an article called a "A Great Case" published in the *New England Journal of Medicine*, a physician reflects:

> *When I became attending physician, I centred ward rounds on great cases. They provided a chance for students to shine, to show off the knowledge they had gained about the pathophysiology of the disease. Great cases also gave interns and residents the opportunity to demonstrate physical findings at the bedside...and gave me a chance to be illuminated in their reflected light.*[37]

Susan Sontag, in a compelling work entitled "Illness as a Metaphor", shows how the disease-centred approach has permeated the language with which diagnoses and treatments are explained to patients.

> *"The controlling metaphors in descriptions of cancer are, in fact, drawn ...from the language of warfare: every physician...is familiar with, if perhaps inured to, this military terminology. Thus cancer cells do not simply multiply they are "invasive"...Cancer cells "colonize"... Rarely are the body's "defenses" vigorous enough...However "radical" the surgical intervention,...the prospects are that "tumor invasion will continue..."*[38]

The metaphor of warfare obviously is far from recognizing that in that body is a person. Her treatise continues: "Treatment also has a military flavour. Radiotherapy uses the metaphors of aerial warfare; patients are 'bombarded' with toxic rays...Treatment aims to 'kill' cancer cells".[39]

Management paradigms, through an effect of inadvertent marketing, have mimicked this metaphor. Risk management and quality are about the "war on errors in medicine". The lack of person in all roles is felt from the patient, to the healthcare clinician, to the management team. The zebra, great case culture and the warfare metaphors all emphasize a patient as a malfunctioning body, and consequently emphasize the disease-centred model of communication. The person physician and the person patient are not considered in the organization and this in turn influences the model with which physicians conduct themselves in their relationships with patients.

The patient-centred model of the physician-patient relationship

The literature suggests that without altering the decision tree that leads to the diagnosis and prescription, it is possible to create a "patient-centred" relationship. This theory suggests that the patient has an agenda and needs a space to describe this to the physician. The proposed complementary relationship central to the disease-centred approach, is not undone; however, the style in which it is managed is changed. According to this theory the non-directed physician-patient encounter allows the physician to diagnose the illness but to hear it in the words of the patient, leaving space for the person in the role of patient. The patient-centred relationship model is considered an improvement on the disease-centred model and not a substitution of it. Is the effectiveness of a patient-centred, or non-directed inquiry with the patient, enough to overcome the complexities of effectively managing the patient?

The patient-centred model of the doctor-patient relationship introduces a variable called "the agenda of the patient". This consists of the patient's ideas and interpretations of the disease, the emotions that the disease generates, the consequence of the disease on the patient's life, and the expectations and desires of the patient. The non-directed doctor-patient visit and open questions allow the physician to make a diagnosis on the one hand and capture the "agenda of the patient" on the other.[40, 41] In this model, both physician and patient have content to contribute to the relationship.

The agenda of the patient, especially in the case of chronic or terminal illness, appears to follow a pattern and consists in phases of acceptance of the diagnosis. The first phase is denial. "This is not happening". The second phase is displacement, meaning getting angry at someone else for what is happening (family member, doctor). The third phase is finding a frame of reference, whether it be spiritual, social or personal in which to reconstruct a world view. The last phase is acceptance, or being able to imagine the consequences of the new state (even death).[42]

The disease-centred approach, which is contained in the model, is conceived as the "agenda of the physician" while in the patient-centred model, the patient is allowed an agenda as well. The patient's agenda is framed as the patient's content in the communication. However, the complementary nature of the relationship coupled with the disease-centred context in which the physician works makes it complicated to understand how to make use of the patient's agenda. In the example of the 60-year old man, who refused to acknowledge his illness, the physician collected the patient's agenda, but was unable to identify how to apply this to the relationship.

In this example, the patient in the role appeared to be in the denial phase of the illness. His problem from a disease-centred perspective was that instead of progressing to accepting his illness he got stuck in the denial phase (phase 1 of 4).

The family asked the doctor for assistance in their relationship with the patient, they did not want their father and husband to die in denial. However, this situation had always been present in the family and never had been managed in the past. They were frustrated with their role and looked to the physician to cure the patient of his denial, as if his denial were the disease, and not the cancer. The family found an ally in the physician because he too was frustrated with the patient's unwillingness to move past denial and meet his own as well as the family's expectations.

The physician who acted in the situation commented on its after-math: "For me this experience remains a moving example of just how wrong things can go, when as a doctor, I think I know what is best for the patient and act accordingly".[43]

In the case discussed above, the patient did not want to hear the diagnosis. He wanted treatment even if these were useless, and he did not accept his condition. The physician who treated this patient used the patient-centred model, he knew that the patient had lost a son and defended his emotional world with denial. However, while every patient has a phase of denial in accepting a terminal illness, this patient has traits of denial in his person. When his son died, he managed it with denial. He himself was terminally ill and managed his disease with denial. This was not a "phase" but his expression as a person.

The physician himself mused afterwards over this case and commented:

> "What I would now criticize in my behavior at the time, however is that I failed to see how strongly the man signalled. Why do we continue to ignore the significance of a person's biographical details?"[44]

The patient-centred model suggests that the patients are satisfied with communicating biographical details, however the part of the model which is not explored is what next? In this case, the physician had the patient communicate biographical details but did not know how to listen to them.

As the physician points out in this case, what was missing was an understanding of the person in the role of patient. The relationship map identifies two dimensions of each participant in the relationship: role and person. Both the physician and the patient are in roles, but are, at the same time, people. As such, the difficulty of forging the doctor-patient relationship lies in forming a focused but sensitive personal relationship within the confines of the different roles assigned to the doctor and the patient. In building the blended relationship with the patient, the principal variable with which physicians must struggle in the passage from the disease-centred to the blended relationship is the "time of the patient". The patient-centred model seeks to establish the best course of action for the patient, but does not contemplate the "time of the patient" in accepting the illness and its consequences. The physician, in order to build an effective relationship with the patient needs to understand the person in the role.

Efforts in understanding the problems of the physician-patient relationship have focused on the content of the relationship, rather than on the proposed relationship.

The data on literacy might initially point to the content of the message as the principal obstacle to a compliant outcome of the doctor-patient relationship. If the patient cannot read and cannot understand, the problem lies in the content of the message and its packaging. However, communication theory suggests that the "proposed relationship" is the principal cause of malfunction in human communication. Taking the same data on patient illiteracy, it is not simply a question of not understanding. Patients are ashamed of speaking openly about illiteracy. An effective proposed relationship will allow them to communicate effectively and manage the information they need.

Furthermore, the fact that self care in chronic disease requires the patient to report changes to the physician, touches some of the principal routines of the "proposed relationship" in the disease-centred model. The patient is asked to spontaneously initiate communication with the physician on the basis of self-care practices, rather than being asked. Hypochondria is a fear of disease, and too often results in endless diagnostic tests. A firm relationship with the physician and the team can reduce the recourse to these useless and sometimes invasive tests. In conclusion by using the person-role model, the proposed relationship is identified as the critical part of the physician-patient relationship.

In a Lancet article, Groopman illustrates the difficulty for physicians of recognizing the person in the role, both for themselves and for the patient. As a physician, he writes patient stories and he comments "when I looked hard at the first drafts I realised that a character was missing. That character was myself... I was reluctant to fill in the void. This reluctance came from my medical training, which taught me that in the therapeutic relationship the physician must mask his or her inner thoughts and emotions. Writing about myself meant revealing what was going on in my head and my heart..."[45]

Management: supporting the physician-patient relationship

Non-compliance is another way of saying that the patient is managing his/her care, not the physician. Predictors of poor compliance indicate that at issue is the doctor-patient relationship. The quantity of information that the patient must absorb correctly, such as medication that interferes with lifestyle, and poor communication with health professionals are all areas that are indicators of the doctor-patient relationship.[46]

The costs of non-compliance are both in terms of health and resources. Non-compliant HIV patients, for example, develop drug resistant strains of the disease that eventually lead to death. The same occurs for other long term treatments like are necessary for tuberculosis. The costs of non-compliance, like the costs of health literacy, are estimated in billions of dollars.

The costs in terms of inappropriate or wasted resources of patient management of the physician-patient relationship amount to estimated hundreds of billions of dollars, according to the data on the various areas of dysfunction. Data on compliance indicates that 50% of patients have "assumed" the management of their health. In non-compliant patients, health status deteriorates. The solution may lie in better doctor-patient communication.

From a management perspective, the health system is largely in the hands of physicians in their individual relationships with their patients. Data indicates the communication skills that they currently possess are insufficient in at least 50% of cases.

Much research has been dedicated to the communication skills of physicians and how to create a relationship where the physician, the expert, is managing the health of the patient. This is not the only lever for managing the runaway "patient manager" of the health system. The blended relationship model can be used to analyse some successful management practices that go beyond "communication skills of the physician". There are interesting cases in point that demonstrate the importance of other management tools, beyond the doctor-patient relationship, in improving the outcomes of healthcare. These tools include organizing for the patient in the role, the medical equipe as people in the role, measuring performance of physicians and patients in the role, identifying aggressive performance goals, managing the "social shame" of physicians and patients as people in the role, and management of the "other person's time". All these examples take existing management tools and adapt them to the specific nature of healthcare.

The role of organization

The doctor-patient relationship, in an inadvertent marketing perspective, is framed within the organization. The nature of relationships within the organization creates a relationship style, which third parties can see and understand. Therefore, the current lack of focus on the person in the role in blended relationships within the organization is a much bigger cause of disease-centred doctor-patient relationships than anyone had acknowledged. Management cannot attribute a 50% failure rate in doctor-patient communication to the lack of communication skills possessed by the "person" doctor. Management of the patient is simply reflecting relationship models in the health system among professionals. The following examples illustrate how the proposed relationship model within the medical community can produce positive outcomes in the health of the patients with an appropriate use of resources.

The case of breastfeeding in maternity wards provides insight into alternatives for "educating health providers" and shows evidence for how organization of the patient's role is an alternative to physician communication as the only managerial lever for managing the "assumed" patient manager. In the 70s the clinical benefits of breastfeeding became evident and led to better health for the child and better psychological health of the mother-child relationship. It was found that some mothers had stopped breastfeeding in the hospital.

The key moment to intervene was the moment the mother had given birth. Health professionals, and especially nurses, were sent to training classes. The purpose of these classes was to improve nurses' communication skills with mothers about the importance of breastfeeding and developing communication techniques to encourage mothers to breastfeed. This investment in improving the communication skills of health workers did not produce the desired outcome of increasing the number of mothers who breastfed when they left the hospital.

Organization of the maternity ward was impeding mothers from breastfeeding their newborns despite its being clinically proven to benefit the health of their babies. In fact, the organization of the maternity ward was not conducive to the content of the messages the nurses were conveying to the new mothers. Maternity wards were organized with nurseries to facilitate the work of the nurses. Nurses brought babies to their mothers' bedsides at fixed times to be nursed. This way, nurses passed an equal amount of time on a number of tasks. The ward was organized in a way that facilitated the job of the nurse.

There was no attention to the "time of the other" in this case, of either the mother or her baby: whether the baby was sleeping, had been hungry, or other variables, like the sleep patterns of the child. Babies whose sleep patterns were disturbed cried instead of eating, and made their mothers anxious that their babies were starving. Generally mothers gave up nursing because in their view it was better for the baby to eat something than breastfeed and eat nothing.

Rooming-in, an organizational solution to the breastfeeding dilemma, radically increased the number of mothers who breastfed. Rooming-in simply reorganized the relationships. The solution had little to do with the communication skills of each nurse, but invoked the organizational capacity to create compliance. Rooming-in placed babies in the room with their mother. Mothers could feed as much or as little as the baby needed. Nurses were available on request if a mother was unsure of how to feed or change her child. Thus, managing the ward was about being there, if there was a mother who requested assistance. Nurses were obliged to work in a team rather than perform duties and activities on an individual basis.

Nothing in the ward changed from a content perspective. Nurses still were responsible for the same professional contents and were still in a complementary relationship with mothers. However, the proposed relationship between caregivers and patients did change by activating the person-role model of care. Mothers and newborns were given a role in the organization.

Learning in groups

The second example concerns the learning curve of physicians in the operating room. When surgeons switch from one operating technique to another, they make mistakes. When surgeons switched from the Senning technique for "blue babies" they increased life expectancy over time from 33 to 47 years. However, in the first 100 operations, studies in 16 different hospitals, demonstrated that mortality increased from 6% with the Senning technique to 25%.[47]

A Harvard Business School study on learning curves in medicine studied the advent of non-invasive heart surgery.[48] The question studied was whether the learning curve was a collective process or an individual one, and if one showed significant differences from the other. The basic question was, does practice make perfect apply to the individual, or can it be improved by working in a group? The results were astounding. The study examined 16 different hospitals as they adopted this new non-invasive surgery technique. The differences in operating time at the 40th case between "the best" and "the average" case was 88 minutes. The best case had reduced operating time from 500 to 132 minutes by case 50. This was quantified as a US $9,000 cost saving per case. Learning was not standard across the 16 hospitals. Learning had a bell curve.

In the best case, one surgeon hand picked the team, sent the team for training and scheduled operations with that team and that team only for the next 15 operations. Six were scheduled in a week so that the learning curve would keep people on the team in focus. In 15 operations, this team halved procedure time. Other learning procedures in this hospital's approach included sharing information with other departments, and a briefing with the team before and after each operation.

Other teams formed randomly by the surgeon on the basis of availability were, in the words of the surgeon in charge, "a disaster".

...there were no meetings to discuss cases ahead of time. An anaesthesiologist noted, "I get no warning of a minimally invasive case until I show up at the hospital". There was also little indication that the staff involved with this procedure viewed themselves as a "team". One nurse noted. "We don't have any real teams here. It's just who gets assigned on any given day".

Another added "The nurses are interchangeable we know our 'little job' and don't really know what the other people are doing".[49]

This case study demonstrates the importance of the blended relationship model in building team membership, and how it matters that the same people stay together to improve the learning curve. In the successful learning curve, the same people were kept in the team to create the learning process, only later were new members added. These people learned their new roles faster. In the average case, learning was thought of as an individual process and no attention was paid to the collective learning experience.

Benchmarking and high performance

The third example concerns measuring outcomes and benchmarking performance. This has nothing to do with respecting clinical protocols and staying in the average; but is a more aggressive performance-driven model of measuring healthcare outcomes.

The Cystic Fibrosis Foundation has recorded data on treatment centres for over 40 years and the data is disconcerting. CF patients had a life expectancy of 10 years in 1966, 18 in 1972 and 33 years in 2003. However, in 2003, at the best centre, it was 47 years and its oldest patient was 64.[50] Again this reveals performance as a bell curve. The Institute for Healthcare Improvement began to track these records and has made them public. With this information, doctors, nurses, hospitals, patients and their families know if they are being treated by a mediocre or a centre of excellence. The Director of the Institute affirms "if we open the book on physician's results, the lessons will be exposed. And if we are genuinely curious about how the best achieve their results... they (information and techniques) will spread."[51]

At the best centre, the following case is reported. An 18-year old patient with CF was breathing at 90% down 19% from her previous visit. This is the record of the physician's visit with her:

"Any cough lately? No. Colds? No. Fevers? No. Was she sure she'd been taking her treatments regularly? Yes, of course. Every day? Yes. Did she ever miss treatments? Sure. Everyone does once in a while. How often is once in a while?

Then slowly Warwick got a different story out of her: in the past few months it turned out she'd barely been taking her treatments at all. He pressed on. 'Why aren't you taking your treatments?' ...He seemed genuinely curious, as if he'd never run across this interesting situation before. 'I don't know'. He kept pushing 'What keeps you from doing your treatments?' I don't know. 'Up here' he pointed at his own head – 'What's going on?' 'I don't know', she said.

He paused... 'Let's look at the numbers' he said. 'A person's daily risk of getting a bad lung illness with CF is 0.5%...The daily risk of getting a bad lung illness with CF plus treatment is 0.05% so when you experiment you're looking at the difference between a 99.95% chance of staying well and a 99.5% chance of staying well. Seems hardly any difference. Right? On any given day you have basically a 100% chance of being well. But...It is a big difference...Sum it up over a year and it is the difference between an 83% chance of making it through 2004 without getting sick and a 16% chance (of not getting sick)'".[52]

By using and sharing the data with the patient on the prognosis, the physician was able to break through her "I don't know" and discover that she had a boyfriend and having to go home and to the school nurse for treatment was embarrassing her. They made a plan to involve her best friend. Her treatment plan involved the actors in her life, and not the places that treatment was being offered.

The doctor is treating the person in the role of patient. As a patient, she should simply "take her medication". As a person in the role, she is 18, an adolescent, who experienced social shame at showing her friends at school that she had to go to the infirmary every day, and home to mom to do her breathing treatments. The physician explored the ways in which she as a person, could function in her role as patient.

The best practice centre uses the data to build the medical team. There is a weekly meeting to establish and share everyone's care. The aim is not to meet the average 80% lung function but to reach 100% or better. This centre does not measure itself against the average, it seeks to create the benchmark. Ironically it follows none of the medical protocols for managing the disease. From a management perspective, this involves identifying only one key indicator of performance, percentage of breathing capacity of the patient. Furthermore, the team is fundamental at all levels; in the patient's compliance and in the centre's performance. Each person, physician, is responsible to the other physicians for the breathing results of each patient. And each person patient, is responsible to each physician for meeting clinical goals: 100% or above. In this case, the simplicity of the information that gets shared is striking. The reporting system uses one indicator of outcome. This is enough to create accountability in the physician-physician relationship as well as in the physician-patient relationship.

When to work with the individual and not with the group

The person in the role and social shame, apply to the physician as much as they do to the patient. In treating hospital-based infection, one hospital took physician social shame into account. A researcher clocked how long physicians washed their hands, which products they used, and charted this against mortality and hospital-based infections. Individual reports were sent to physicians in which they could see their habits, as compared to others, and their performance as compared to others. Nobody in the surgical team, except the physician himself, knew who the worst performer was. Poor performers were motivated to improve performance by calling and getting information as to the most successful ways of avoiding infections. Secondary hospital-based infections as well as mortality dropped significantly as a result.

The last example illustrates the importance of the role-person model in managing a "near miss" malpractice suit. This case is described by a German physician, and exemplifies many of the issues involved in the patient's "assumption" of the management role in the health system in malpractice cases.

Kristen and Frode's children were three and seven years old. The three-year old knocked over a saucepan of boiling water. The consequence was a minor third degree burn. During his first days at the hospital the situation was completely under control. Then one morning he was found in his bed, pale, unconscious, and without a palpable pulse. His condition was rapidly perceived to be septic shock (acute blood poisoning), a sudden and unexpected complication. Despite intensive and exhaustive treatment, he was declared brain dead three days later. The parents were informed that their son was brain dead. Additionally they were told that we considered it appropriate to switch off the artificial respirator. The parents were in a state of deep shock. The situation was not made any easier by the fact that on their initial arrival at the hospital they had been told that the burns were not life threatening...When I explained that unforeseen complications had led to the child becoming brain dead, and that we could say with certainty that there was no possibility of the brain functioning again, their reaction came as a shock to me. After a few minutes the mother said, "you know that I have money. I will hire the best lawyer in the world. I will pursue you to hell and back if you attempt to shut down the respirator". [53]

The physician involved concentrated on the biological and practical facts of the case in his approach to communicating with the mother of the brain dead child. The child was brain dead, the respirator was being used for no tangible clinical purpose and therefore it was appropriate, from the physician's and a health system's management perspective, to convey the situation and shut down the respirator. The situation had taken an ugly turn, but from a content perspective, was objectively, a "closed case".

The mother of the child faced two emotional situations. The first was grief. The loss of a child is a lifelong source of grief for a parent. However, her reaction towards the physician was of anger "I will pursue you to hell and back if you attempt to shut down the respirator". Her anger was directed to the doctor's request to shut down the respirator. Her anger was about her moment of grief being treated with such insensitivity to the person in the role. Her grief is beginning for her lifetime, and the physician is concerned with the respirator. Anger is an emotion of limited duration but if fed, can last a long time.

Who is managing the respirator in the hospital at this point? If the physician continues to perceive the respirator as his or a hospital "resource" this could lead to other attempts to persuade the mother to shut down the respirator. As a consequence of the doctor-patient relationship, the respirator was no longer a resource managed by the hospital: but now managed by the mother. If her anger is fed, she will indeed begin a lawsuit as she has threatened. This will be at a huge monetary cost to the hospital, and will also jeopardize the use of the respirator for an indefinite period of time. This situation can be analysed using the blended relationship model.

At issue is a mother, role and person who has lost a child, rather than a "brain dead child". A parent who has just lost a child unexpectedly cannot be expected to objectively evaluate the way a respirator is being used. In this case, the damage has occurred; the physician sent two messages in one: the patient is dead, the respirator is ours.

By using the blended relationship model, it is possible to understand that the mother's grief will last a lifetime but not directed at the physician or the respirator. The mother's anger at seeing her physician speak of her dead three-year old son as another case, and the respirator as a resource, is palpable. Her refusal to accept this role in the relationship and execute the physician's orders was made explicit with her threat to take the whole matter to court. When the doctor-patient relationship model is no longer accepted by the patient, this is often the moment that the patient assumes power in the relationship by menacing a lawsuit or simply claiming resources. Management, is in fact based, on the management of the patient relationship.

At this point, when the doctor-patient relationship has collapsed because the patient refuses it, management is about doing nothing and waiting for the relationship to improve. The reconstruction of the relationship depends on the "time of the other person in the other role", in this case, the mother's time. Anger may be short lived in one person and longer lived in another. To manage is defined as: to handle, to direct, to make and keep submissive, to alter by manipulation. Time of the other person is a very frustrating concept in the management paradigm because there is nothing to direct, it is about waiting. It is counter-intuitive that management of critical situations in healthcare may be more about doing nothing than doing something.

In this case, any management activities on the part of the physician or the hospital will feed the mother's anger. The mother is a person in a role and needs at this point some time to cool down. Management of the mother will be accomplished only by not handling, not manipulating and not keeping submissive.

The case in point describes how doctor-patient relationships are the core of managing health systems. The physician describes the outcome of this case.

> "They sat with their child for three days. In this time they did not want to speak to me. Then I was told that the mother had broken down in the night. The next day they came to see me and said 'you can turn the respirator off now'".[54]

It was the mother who had the best managerial solution at the lowest cost to the hospital. The mother decided when to shut down the respirator which only nominally belongs to the hospital. The cost of a poorly managed relationship with the patient is that health system resources are managed by patients and their families.

The case in point evidences that in the event of an "error" or poor communication, the best course of action, as delineated by the blended relationship model is waiting for the "time of the other", and consists in management doing nothing at all.

Conclusion

All these examples show the importance of person in a role, not only patients but also physicians. The blended relationship between physicians, and the acknowledgement that physicians, like their patients, are people in the role, is fundamental for managing patient care inside the health system. Each case illustrated in the previous paragraphs builds a management model on the basis of the model.

The first case, of rooming-in, puts the person mother in a role with the newborn, and the nurses offer technical assistance on request. In this case, the patient's role is reinforced by the organizational model. In the second case, the importance of a collective learning process is emphasized. Teams do not learn quickly unless the same people work together on a problem and work together to understand where they can improve. The person in the role is fundamental. It is not enough to put together a surgical team, but team members must know one another and share their learning. The third case evidences that communication with the non-compliant patient is no easy task. However, if the physician, in turn, has to respond to his/her colleagues in the hospital concerning his patients' performance, the motivation to understand the issues of non-compliance is driven by the physician's accountability to the professional team. Furthermore, the person in the role of patient has to determine how to achieve compliance with the assistance of the physician. The hospital-based infection case demonstrates that just as patient's live the diversity of being illiterate with social shame, so the physician lives error with social shame. As in the case of secondary, hospital-based infections, a management system that accepts social shame and hides the identity of non-performers from colleagues can induce the person in the role to seek help rather than defend the role. Lastly, in the event of a conflict between a physician and a patient, the best course of action, according to the person-role model, is to give the person-patient time to cool off and reconstruct the relationship. Anger in relationship management is the principal cause of malpractice suits. This introduces a new management technique for crisis situations: doing nothing.

As these examples point out, management tools are extremely useful in the doctor-patient relationship. However, they need to be adjusted to the particular nature of the problem or objective at hand. The blended relationship is a management tool for understanding physician-patient communication and conflict. Solutions, on the other hand, need to be suited to the setting.

3
The Non-cooperative Game, the Nash Theory of Equilibrium and Healthcare Management

Non-cooperative games and the healthcare organization

In his Nobel prize winning work, John Nash observed relationships from a mathematical and economic perspective. He was interested in relationships not only between people, but between organizations, and countries. In the previous chapters, this book has observed relationships between people in organizations, Nash observed what he termed transactions between parties. He called the relationships that developed from the observation of these transactions "games". Game theory studies relationships from a different perspective, and uses different terms to describe the same issues. Briefly, in translation, games are relationships, transactions are agreements and actions, parties are the actors in the relationship.

When John Nash was doing his work, game theory had already identified what was known as a cooperative game. A cooperative game is defined as a relationship between parties where the agreements (transactions) made between two parties are guaranteed by a third, outside, party. Cooperative games got their name because the parties engaging in the relationship were cooperative with one another when a third party was guaranteeing their agreements. In fact, the role of the third party turned out to be more of a presence than an active party. The mere presence of the third party acted to enforce reciprocal cooperation between the parties themselves.

One example of a cooperative game is a commercial contract between parties designed to be honoured under the law. If one of the parties does not respect the terms of the contract, the other can turn to the legal system (outside party) to enforce cooperation. The consequences of non-collaboration, costly lawsuits, for example, make it opportune for each party to respect the terms of the agreement. These agreements are easily self-enforceable because working backwards, it is in no party's best interest to defect from the agreement, because the sanction will be enforced by the third party under the terms and conditions of the contract. In conclusion, it is not so much the actions of the third party but the mere existence of this outside party that encourages the players to respect their original agreement.

John Nash appreciated the mathematics of cooperative games, however he observed that many transactions between parties, did not have a designated outside party in the role of guarantor so that the parties would be motivated to respect their agreements. This situation, where two parties enter into a transaction, and have no third party to guarantee that they will collaborate, was defined by Nash as a non-cooperative game.

A non-cooperative game sounds like a game where there is no cooperation between players. However, this is not what the term means. A non-cooperative game is a game in which players make contracts that are only enforceable through reciprocal cooperation. There is no third party to enforce the contract between the players and so players self-enforce their collaborative efforts.[55] This is the distinguishing characteristic of a non-cooperative game. In a non-cooperative game achieving an optimal outcome in the transaction between parties depends on self-enforced cooperative behaviour. Peer to peer relationships, described in the previous chapters, look like a non-cooperative game.

This chapter will explore the possibility that the management of the healthcare system resembles the management of a non-cooperative game. If this were to be the case, the management of the healthcare system would have to focus on tools which reinforce reciprocal cooperation inside the organization. This way of looking at healthcare management could shed more light on its nature. The non-cooperative game will be examined in the healthcare organization with an approach known as the indirect proof. Von Neumann and Morgenstern describe this process as follows:

> This consists of imagining that we have a satisfactory theory of a certain desired type, trying to picture the consequences of this imaginary situation and then in drawing conclusions from this as to what the hypothetical theory must be like in detail. If this process is applied successfully, it may narrow down the possibilities for the hypothetical theory of the type in question to such an extent that only one possibility is left – i.e. that the theory is determined.[56]

This chapter will explore the nature of a non-cooperative game, the equilibrium of a non-cooperative game (Nash equilibrium) and will examine some examples from healthcare management to support the hypothesis that healthcare management may indeed look like a non-cooperative game. This would imply that healthcare could function more successfully by focusing on bolstering self-enforcing cooperation. Theories of negotiation will be explored as important tools for strengthening the relationship between players in a non-cooperative game.

Many healthcare management issues in fact depend on self-enforcing collaborative efforts between players in the organization. An example of the self-enforced collaborative contract in healthcare management can be drawn from an 1,100-bed teaching hospital in New York, where clinical departments were challenged by operations management in the budget process to reduce patient length of stay.

> The Clinical Department's ability to achieve reduced length of stay depended in part on optimizing its internal organization, but also on collaboration with other departments. Specifically, the longest length of stay cases were cases passed from the Emergency Room to the Department of Medicine with no confirmed diagnosis, these patients were too critical to be sent home, and were sent to the Department to define their health problem. These patients inevitably accumulated long periods of hospitalization as they required frequent tests and visits off the floor in order to obtain a diagnosis. As they were often off the floor, they missed meals and lost weight; consequently, their health condition worsened. Some patients lost more weight from missed meals and errors in the kitchen than they did from their illness.[57] The capacity to manage these cases more effectively depended on creating better links between the Department of Medicine and other departments such as radiology, the kitchen, and the laboratory, for example.
>
> Management had negotiated objectives with each department separately. The focus of each department was on its own self-interest.

The Nash theory of equilibrium and the prisoner's dilemma

In order to illustrate the theoretical ideas behind Nash's work, the prisoner's dilemma will be used as an example of a non-cooperative game. In the prisoner's dilemma two people are arrested as suspected partners in a crime. Each is put into a separate cell and given two options: to confess or to stay mum. If one of the two confesses and the other stays mum, the one who confesses will have partnered with the justice system and will be released from jail, while the one who stays mum will receive the full punishment. If both confess, both will receive a reduced sentence for having partnered with the justice system. If both stay mum, there is not enough information to indict either partner and both will be released from jail. In the prisoner's dilemma there is no third party to enforce cooperation between the prisoners themselves. Each prisoner will have to work on his/her own strategy, and payoffs or punishments will result from the other prisoner's strategy, no third party will intervene.

Rationally, the best outcome of the prisoner's dilemma is that the two prisoners stay mum (cooperate with one another) and this way neither serves a jail sentence. However, the nature of a non-cooperative game has to do with the fact that this cooperation has to be self-enforced. In order to achieve the optimal outcome, each has to trust that the other will cooperate (stay mum) and not defect (confess). However, if each person takes into account his own and the other's best interest, neither will cooperate. How does this paradox, where rational thinking produces a suboptimal outcome, actually work?

In considering how to behave, each prisoner must take into account the choices available to the other prisoner. If I am one of the two prisoners, in thinking about my choices, I think that he is thinking about my thinking, and I am taking into account my thinking about his thinking and vice versa.

This leads each prisoner to focus on his best choice: if I stay mum (cooperate with the other prisoner), and he confesses, I lose, whereas if I confess and he stays mum (cooperates with me) then I win. If my partner keeps mum, then I go free whatever I do, whereas if my partner confesses, I'm better off confessing myself. Therefore, it is not in my best interest to cooperate, because I can be sure that it is in his best interest to confess. The other player does the same.

The strategy "both prisoners cooperate with one another" is unstable as a player could do just as well, if not better, by defecting while the other player still cooperates. An equilibrium is a situation in which if I take a position my situation remains stable, or gets better, regardless of what the other player does. Therefore, the strategy "both cooperate" (both prisoners stay mum) is not an equilibrium. It is not an equilibrium because it is unstable, in this position each party's situation is unstable, because a move on the part of the other player will make my situation worse. Even when a negotiation has occurred between the prisoners, this continues to be true. If I continue to cooperate, my situation can get worse if the other player does not respect the negotiation. The fear of the other prisoner's "best move" still means that neither knows if they can truly trust the other. The equilibrium of the prisoner's dilemma is that each confess. Table 3.1 illustrates the dilemma.[58]

While the self-enforced cooperation (both stay mum) produces the best outcome, the equilibrium of this non-cooperative game is that

Table 3.1   The prisoner's dilemma

Prisoner 1	Prisoner 2	Result for Prisoner 1	Result for Prisoner 2
Stay mum (cooperate with the other prisoner)	Stay mum (cooperate with the other prisoner)	Get out of jail	Get out of jail
Stay mum (cooperate with the other prisoner)	Confess (defect)	Get a long prison sentence	Get out of jail
Confess (defect)	Stay mum (cooperate with the other prisoner)	Get out of jail	Get a long prison sentence
Confess (defect)	Confess (defect)	Get a reduced sentence	Get a reduced sentence

both confess and get a reduced sentence. It is an equilibrium because if the prisoner chooses confess, the situation is defined by a reduced sentence, and if the other prisoner were to stay mum, the situation will improve because the prisoner would get out of jail. Nash was able to prove that the system would stabilize at its equilibrium point, and the equilibrium point in this game would be non-cooperation. Each prisoner is certain that from the equilibrium point, if they stay in their position, their situation can get better but not worsen. Therefore, it was possible to predict the outcome of a non-cooperative game like the prisoner's dilemma by determining its equilibrium which was the point of greatest stability for each player and does not necessarily coincide with the optimal outcome for both players. This point of greatest stability is called the Nash equilibrium in a non-cooperative game.[59]

If there is a set of strategies for a game with the characteristic that no player can gain advantage from changing his strategy if the other player keeps his strategy unchanged, that set of strategies is originating from Nash equilibrium. In the Nash equilibrium, players fail to see that their self-interest will be realized within the best interests of the group. "There are situations in economics or international politics in which, effectively, a group of interests are involved in a non-cooperative game without being aware of it: the non-awareness helping to make the situation truly non-cooperative".[60]

While self-interest would lead each player to determine a set of strategies independently of the other players, the non-cooperative game indicates the dynamic quality of strategy. Strategy will be developed around the predicted behaviour of the other players.[61] However, predicted behaviour of the other players is also reasoned in terms of self-interest. The entire transaction fails to see the collective advantage of cooperation. Therefore, a non-cooperative game does not mean that an optimal outcome does not exist. It means that the optimal outcome may not coincide with the most stable solution.

The outcomes of healthcare organizations look like Nash equilibrium of the prisoner's dilemma. That is to say, the most stable outcomes are not the optimal outcomes. Cooperative mechanisms are self-enforcing in the organization and this defines the organization as a non-cooperative game. Furthermore, a more careful analysis of the healthcare organization identifies that optimal outcomes are not stable outcomes. The system will tend towards stable over optimal outcomes following the Nash theory of equilibrium. Optimal results, therefore, are difficult to achieve because the healthcare organization is a non-cooperative game where stability and positive outcomes are not one and the same.

A self-enforcing cooperation in the healthcare organization therefore depends on recognizing one's own best interest in the context of the best interest of the group.

To return to the example cited previously:

The Department of Medicine negotiated reduced length of stay objectives with management. This was a one on one negotiation between management and the Department of Medicine. However, the most critical length of stay cases could objectively be managed better only if the patient moved efficiently between departments. An objective of reduced length of stay for the Department of Medicine when measured on the length of stay of the single admission did not encourage self-enforced cooperation between the Department of Medicine and other departments. The Department of Medicine negotiated objectives with management that lay outside of the department's control without negotiating with other departments to guarantee that the result was obtainable. Undesirable consequences of this budget objective which occurred, included multiple admissions of a patient for a single health episode to reduce apparent length of stay, while the possibility to reduce length of stay for the health episode remained untapped. An objective of reduced length of stay for the Department of Medicine if measured on the length of stay of the single admission, is not encouraging cooperation between the Department of Medicine and other departments.

The self-interest of the Department of Medicine in meeting budget objectives created negative consequences both for the hospital as a whole as well as for the department itself. There is a saying in engineering that says if you can't measure it you can't do it, if you can't measure it right, you can't do it right. This outcome could be read as Nash equilibrium of the non-cooperative hospital budget system.

In this example, the specific nature of healthcare management is pinpointed. Management's goal was to reduce length of stay; however, it did not steer the players away from the "stable" solution and towards a positive outcome solution, by increasing the incentive to cooperate.

The problem in the Department of Medicine involves identifying an indicator that will encourage self-enforced cooperation with other Departments. In this case, reduced length of stay could be translated into an indicator of turnover time in the patient care process between departments. Requiring limited turnover times every time the patient leaves the floor, would in fact be a decisive determinant of length of stay. This type of indicator would reinforce a cooperative behaviour in a non-cooperative game. Management would obtain reduced length of stay, however management objectives would focus on stimulating cooperation.

Exploring examples of optimal and suboptimal outcomes in healthcare

Some examples of the non-cooperative game in the healthcare system follow. These examples highlight where management intervened to encourage self-enforced collaboration, obtaining an optimal outcome, and where management instead, left the players to assume the Nash equilibrium as it occurs in the non-cooperative game, where stability determines a suboptimal outcome. The examples examine different levels of the system: doctor-patient, doctor-doctor, department-department, Local Health Authority and Hospital. The attention to managing the non-collaborative nature of the relationship is not systematic, and therefore seems to have developed casually. All the managerial actions described have produced optimal outcomes because they bolstered self-enforcing collaboration. The non-collaborative game and Nash equilibrium are useful tools in understanding why an outcome was a success or a failure in healthcare management.

The general practitioner in Italy is a figure who traditionally bolstered self-enforced collaboration in the family over health issues. This figure used to be called "the family doctor". The following case study, told by a GP in a small Piedmont community illustrates the social-clinical nature of the GP in the Italian community, and how the GP works to encourage cooperation in a non-cooperative game.

I am a GP in the Piedmont region, in a rural area. I have been in this community my whole working life. Last year, a woman, about sixty years old, came to see me in my office. She came to me asking for help in tears.

She and her husband live on their farmland, and have two children, who studied at university, have grown up and moved away to the city. Her husband had always been a heavy drinker and had at times become violent. Recently, his episodes of violence had become more frequent.

I did a physical examination of the patient and found her badly bruised and in a terrible psychological condition. Under the circumstances, the law required me to file a police report and request a restraining order on the husband. If I were to have seen the patient and not undertaken this process, in the eventuality of a homicide, I would have been an accomplice and punished under the law. I explained to her that under the circumstances, I was required to file a police report.

She protested vehemently and begged me not to do so. She explained that her husband was a good man, and that in the morning, when he had sobered up, he would beg her pardon. It was the drinking that was ruining him. I thought about the situation and asked her if she thought she could persuade her husband to come see me. She said that she was sure she could. However, it would only be the next day.

When she left my office, I walked over to the police department and without filing a report, explained to the commanding officer, whom I have known for years, what my plan was. In the eventuality that the husband did not come to see me, the commanding officer promised to drive over and have a "friendly chat" with him in order to help me get to see him. The next morning the husband presented himself in my office. I asked him if he would be willing to undergo alcohol treatment. He was willing.

I hospitalized him for ten days to detoxify him and to facilitate his success in an Alcoholics Anonymous group. I also reasoned that ten days for the wife at home alone, would give her the time to recover physically and psychologically so that she could support him in his treatment program. Two years have passed and he has completely stopped drinking.

This account demonstrates the general practitioner's role in the community. The first question to examine here is "who is the patient?" In this doctor's account, while the patient was apparently the wife, in reality it was the couple, husband and wife. The physician's decision to hospitalize the husband, rather than the wife is extremely interesting. The GP examined the best solution for the health of this family, not of the wife separate from her family. He helped the couple identify that the best outcome and the stability of their relationship lay in working together on a solution. The husband and wife are in a non-cooperative game. A positive outcome of their dilemma is possible; however, it involved helping them to self-enforce collaboration.

The physician listened to the woman, not only in her physical distress but in her social distress, and identified a solution that would encourage the couple to cooperate with one another. He understood that a 60-year old woman who put a restraining order on her husband in the community would undergo a process of social shame that could lead to brutal consequences. Furthermore, he identified the best place for each to recover: the husband in the hospital where he will be forced to not drink, and the wife at home, where she lived. As for the legal implications of the case, the GP protected himself with an informal chat with the chief of police who was willing to take a supporting role in the process. He supported the couple to identify a positive outcome in a non-collaborative game.

The professional identity of a GP in a rural context becomes very clear: the GP manages social shame, the health of the family, an informal interorganizational network, and ultimately supports the self-enforced cooperation in the non-cooperative family dynamic.

General practitioners in Italy are paid on a per-capita basis by the State. Each patient whom the GP has contributes to his/her income directly. On the other hand, Local Health Authorities (LHAs) must use their per-capita budgets to pay for all healthcare of acute and non-acute patients. In the city of Milan, for example, the LHA is responsible for 850 GPs and their spending. Managing nearly one thousand GPs who are not paid by the LHA, but who are spending LHA resources is certainly a difficult task. Just to give an idea of how much GPs' behaviour influences the budget, in the LHA of Piacenza, 53% of the operating budget is spent on non-acute care.

The specific characteristics of the GP role have been largely ignored by LHA management. In interpreting the data generated by the case described above, management would have found a ten-day hospitalization an inappropriate allocation of resources for an alcoholic. However, if the health of the population was measured as the outcome of the non-cooperative game, a greater understanding of general medicine and its role in reenforcing self-care behaviours would generate a different analysis of this case. However, currently management is focused on controlling GP behaviour and spending after it has happened.

One area of LHA management is pharmaceutical prescriptions and diagnostic tests in non-acute patients, and their costs to the system. From the LHA's perspective, GPs generate disproportionate costs in terms of pharmaceuticals, diagnostic tests, and hospitalization that must be paid for from resources available to the LHA to manage the health of the population.

Management wondered how to know if these resources were being used well, especially because of the variability in GP's spending behaviour. This was true even adjusting the patient base of each GP by weighting the health situation of the patients enrolled. As a result, given the same complexity of the patient base, GPs' spending behaviour were inconsistent.

As a consequence, management in LHA designed pharmaceutical budgets for GPs which report back to each GP how much he/she is spending on prescriptions and indicates average GP spending in the LHA. Furthermore, economic incentives were given to GPs who met targeted spending objectives. These reports were management control techniques, they control, after the fact, how much GPs have spent on their patients.

The assumptions behind the budget system were that GPs work alone in offices and that their different approaches to spending were due to non-adherence to clinical guidelines because of their isolated working environment. Teams of GPs were set up to study appropriate guidelines from a clinical perspective. GPs reacted very badly to budgeting and discussing clinical guidelines as it felt to them as if management had judged them of non-professional behaviour and was trying to control them. GPs insisted that they know perfectly well what clinical guidelines suggest; however, the model did not take into account what they termed "the difficult patient".

The difficult patient is the patient that decides what he/she wants and asks the GP to do the paper work. Internet, TV shows and other forms of information (what my friend is prescribed) have made patients aware of what they want. GPs insist they do not like to inappropriately over-prescribe medication or diagnostic exams based on requests from their patients; however, each GP fears that a "no" to an insistent patient's request might mean the patient will turn elsewhere. As each GP defines his/her own best interests, he/she fails to act in the best interests of the group of GPs. The critical management issue, as illustrated by the examples that follow, is how to nurture self-enforcing cooperation among GPs.

The following is a story from a GP in the Province of Milan:

> Ms. Domenica is 30 years old, and has always been anxious about her health. Four years ago during her first and only pregnancy she began to develop hypochondriac behaviours. Her son was born with a slight genetic malformation that was immediately and successfully corrected with surgery. After having gotten a sunburn at the beach, Ms. Domenica turned to a dermatologist, who confirmed that her skin irritation was indeed a sunburn. However, during the visit, the specialist mentioned that these symptoms could sometimes be connected to a more complex situation. Alarmed, Ms. Domenica turned to me, her GP, and requested more information and diagnostic tests. The biochemical exams revealed a small positive for ANA. Not convinced by the reassurance I offered that she had nothing but a sunburn, she insisted that I provide her with referrals to specialists for further testing. This story continued for two years when I finally suggested that she go to a University Hospital to get the ultimate verdict and definitively stop this health odyssey. The University Professor confirmed that she had no existing illness. She then returned to me, affirming that she was sicker than ever as she had self-diagnosed herself with an incurable disease, Sclerodermia.

The GP found himself in the prisoner's dilemma: if he said no to Ms. Domenica who was intent on being sick, she might have changed her GP. In the meantime, despite his diagnosis of wellness he spent LHA resources for two years on diagnostic tests and specialist exams. Why did he do this? The patient had an alternative to accepting the diagnosis: change GP. As this physician reasoned, the other GP would find it in his/her best interests to say "yes" to Ms. Domenica. After all, the new GP would have a new patient in his patient base and earn a larger salary. While GPs report that they over-spend because of the difficult patient, this example suggests that they do so because they are in a non-cooperative game with one another. Each GP fears that if he were to insist and deny the patient access to further testing, then the patient would turn to another GP, and each GP is convinced that another GP would treat her.

The stability of the situation is given by keeping Ms. Domenica and spending resources for her tests and medicines. The positive outcome of this situation would be for her to be denied treatment for her imaginary illness. Stability and positive outcome lie on different planes. The positive outcome lies in the strength of the cooperative relationship between GPs, while the stable outcome lies in keeping the patient.

This reasoning has brought the physician in question to allow his patient to contest his diagnosis for two years. This is the Nash equilibrium at play. The physician has allowed the patient to contest his diagnosis, in a costly manner. The patient underwent unnecessary tests. The LHA has spent resources to no avail. The physician is afraid that another GP will behave as he has behaved allowing the patient to research indefinitely her good health status. Given that the patient is not going to change her strategy, it is not advantageous for the physician to change his. In the absence of self-enforced collaboration among GPs this will continue to create a pocket of unnecessary spending and inappropriate care. GPs are not encouraged to see the best interest of their professional group, and this determines their consequent strategy: self-interest in keeping the patient.

Nash's model of the non-cooperative game allows management to pinpoint the real area of need: GPs chose stability over positive outcomes because their diffidence towards each other makes it evident that maintaining a costly relationship is a more positive outcome than letting it go. Managing GPs needs to focus on encouraging self-enforced cooperation among GPs.

This dynamic can be seen in even larger proportions with the attempt to create group practices. National contracts economically encouraged GPs to form group practices. A GP in group practice with 1,500 patients could earn 4.5 Euros more per patient than if they work alone. This was an economic incentive of up to 6,750 Euros per year per GP. The economic value of the incentive was large. The expected outcome was to reduce non-acute visits to the emergency room. The contract stipulated that group practices had to operate for six hours a day, members of the group practice had to share clinical charts on a common information system allowing the patient to rotate amongst the practitioners. Group practice also stipulated that the group had to produce clinical guidelines for treating chronic illness, etc. For patients this was to mean easy access to their GP's office, a higher quality service, more flexibility, the possibility of receiving a second consultation immediately and other benefits.

In a study conducted in 2000 on the real contents of group practice in the Province of Milan, 84.4% of the group practices did not allow patients to rotate between physicians and none created professional seminars within the group. In describing the principal disadvantages associated with group practice 53.1% cited the difficulty of managing relationships with the other members of the group, and 18.8% cited the "difficult patient".[62] The physicians belonging to a group practice did not trust one another enough to share patients. In this case, while negotiation could take place, if it did, it was ineffective. In fact, the new contract was enforced "literally" but not as intended. Literally the office was open six hours, however, seen from the patient's point of view, he/she could only access the office when his/her physician was there.

One interpretation of these results is that the state contract created a non-cooperative game. There was no way to enforce the spirit of the contract from the outside. The group practice had to be based on self-enforced cooperation among its members. As no tools existed for facilitating this, the group practice was a non-cooperative game and the suboptimal outcome achieved resembles the Nash equilibrium for this type of game. Using this metaphor as a working hypothesis, the issue becomes managing self-enforcing cooperation. This could lead to some interesting ideas for how to more effectively manage the GP role in achieving the desired outcomes from the group practice.

The healthcare organization can be likened to a non-cooperative game and therefore tends towards the suboptimal equilibrium typical of games like the prisoner's dilemma where a stable outcome does not coincide with the optimal outcome. The role of management in the organization in this hypothesis is about nurturing self-enforcing cooperation. The specific nature of healthcare management, discussed in the previous chapter, in addition to the person-role model and its importance, would be that it concerns the management of a non-cooperative game. If this were true, management control, by focusing on controling how resources are consumed, would only be observing ex-post the unfavourable Nash equilibrium, rather than favouring or supporting a more positive outcome by sustaining self-enforced cooperation. In fact, pharmaceutical budgets for GPs do indeed appear to report Nash equilibrium.

Instead, if healthcare organizations do mimic non-cooperative games, management efforts would need to focus on strengthening self-enforcing cooperation in the organization. All forms of suboptimal outcomes in a non-cooperative game are based on roles acting in self-interest while discounting the interests of the group which includes, in the healthcare arena, professionals and patients. In order to produce positive outcomes, healthcare management would have to focus on how to nurture self-enforcing collaboration within the organization. In practical terms, this would mean identifying the interests of the group, and the best outcome for the individual in this context.

Examples of management tools and how they can be used to foster win-win outcomes in non-cooperative games

The examples of successful management experiences, the role of the GP in the community and family, rooming-in, learning curves for new procedures, best practice and hospital-based infection control, explored in the previous chapter can be reread in this light. All these examples nurtured self-enforcing collaboration and helped players see that the best outcome for the individual must take into account the best outcome for the group.

Maternity wards, prior to the advent of rooming-in, asked the nursing staff to self-enforce collaboration. They did this by creating an organizational design that divided the work fairly. The nursery enabled nurses to divide the tasks equally among themselves. Therefore, each nurse acted in an organization where the self-interest of each component was protected; however the outcome was suboptimal because mothers did not leave the hospital breastfeeding. The nursery organization did not take into consideration that the best interest of each party lay in recognizing the best interests of the group: nurses, newborns and mothers. This configuration would look like the win-win solution of the prisoner's dilemma.

This organization was built on "what best interest of the other nurse would be". The nursery and fixed feeding times guaranteed that work was distributed equally between nurses. However, while this risk was controlled through the organization, nurses achieved a non-optimal outcome by focusing exclusively on their own self-interest rather than identifying the collective objectives of the group: encouraging mothers to breastfeed, increasing newborn health status, and professionally gratifying the nurses. It was a Nash equilibrium.

Rooming-in was an organizational solution which promoted self-enforced collaboration between the mother and her newborn, the nurses and the mother, and among the nurses themselves. Organization of work self-enforced collaboration between the players at all levels. In this specific case, the decentralization of the nursery to the mother's bedside strengthened a group effort to achieve win-win outcomes.

Learning curves for new surgical procedures also focused on an organization more geared to protect self-interest than collective interests. The less successful groups did not attribute any value to group learning. Each individual was entitled to training or to shifts which they had negotiated on the basis of self-interest. This meant that new surgical procedures were learned individually and not collectively. The results were longer procedure times and longer learning curves for physicians. If the members of the organization are focused on self-interest and are not encouraged to work as a group, they will fail to see that they are in a non-cooperative game and that they are choosing the Nash equilibrium of that game. As a consequence, the outcomes they achieve are suboptimal. Like the prisoner's dilemma, their best outcome depends on considering the best outcome of the group. The most successful group worked together as a group and organized training and shifts so as to learn together. The Harvard project demonstrated that the best outcome for the individual was associated with his/her belonging to a group.

Cystic fibrosis centres that did not encourage collaboration among physicians by identifying the collective best interest, produced sub-optimal outcomes or high national mortality averages for the disease. However, the most successful clinic treating cystic fibrosis used management indicators to self-enforce collaboration between physicians. The management indicator, respiratory capacity of each patient, enabled physicians to share results and be accountable for his/her individual behaviour to the group. This benefited physicians and patients as both achieved optimal therapeutic outcomes.

In trying to curb hospital-based infections, those hospitals which disclosed such infections of surgical divisions to groups of physicians rather than to individual professionals did not achieve results. Each physician is geared towards defending their professional performance (self-interest) towards colleagues rather than to making changes in their behaviour. Informing individual physicians about their performance in the group encouraged physicians to seek help in learning to reduce hospital-based infections. On the other hand, informing individual GPs of their spending in the group of GPs did not change behaviour. This is because GPs were afraid of losing patients, they knew that they were being inconsistent from a clinical perspective. These contradictory findings show that there is no one miracle managerial tool that will work in healthcare. The specific management action necessary to encourage self-enforcing collaboration has to be designed with great attention to the specificity of the problem. While groups can accelerate the learning curves of new surgical practices, they can slow the learning in a situation where physicians risk the social shame of being exposed to the group.

By analysing examples of both optimal and suboptimal outcomes it becomes evident that success seems to depend on nurturing self-enforcing collaboration, while failure seems a consequence of not having undertaken any concrete action to bolster collaboration. Failure often looks very much like Nash equilibrium of the prisoner's dilemma: failure is the choice of stability over the optimal outcome, where the two do not coincide. These examples indicate a need to identify a systematic approach to healthcare management which nurtures self-enforcing collaboration within and between organizations.

Organization, creating groups, and outcome indicators can all be used to enhance self-enforcing collaboration. In addition to these management tools, negotiation theory is applicable in the context of healthcare management. Since non-cooperative games depend on self-enforced cooperation, and each party is thinking about the best move of the other and determining his/her own behaviour as a consequence, negotiation becomes a way to structure and strengthen relationships.

Negotiation theory as a tool for building relationships in the non-cooperative game

Negotiation theory provides insight into managing negotiation processes in non-cooperative games and into indicators of successful agreements. A negotiation is defined as a two-way communication process with the objective of reaching an agreement. A successful negotiation is an agreement that satisfies the interests of the negotiating parties to the greatest degree possible, is long lasting, reached within the time frames of the negotiating parties, and it should improve or at least not damage the relationship between the negotiating parties.[63]

Negotiation theory has studied two forms of negotiation: position negotiation and interest-based negotiation.

A position is a quantification of an interest on behalf of both parties. It is a single possible solution that will satisfy my interest. For example, in the open market a rug vendor would price the value of the rug and the potential client would offer a price. The compromise reached by the two parties would depend on the power of each party in the transaction. Most negotiations are position negotiations.

Power in the transaction is defined by the player with "a best alternative to a negotiated agreement". That means that if one of the two could afford to not sell or not buy the consequent agreement would lean towards the demands of the party with the best alternative to a negotiated agreement. In theory, the player with the best alternative could impose his price on the other. Another factor in position negotiation is time: how much time it takes to reach the agreement can affect the players in the negotiation differently. An established large organization can afford to fight a long battle, while a fledgling organization will have less resources, less credit and less reputation to survive a price war over time. The importance of time can also be seen in labour negotiations. Workers can strike against employers, however, the player that can outlast the other player is the one that can impose his/her position. Workers may be able to sustain a strike for a year, however, if the employer has time to wait it out, the workers' position will weaken as time goes on or vice versa, if workers can wait it out for a year, and the employer can afford only to wait ten days, the employers' situation weakens.

In addition, negotiation theory identifies psychological aspects to position negotiation. These involve the link between the person and his/her position. Giving in completely to the other negotiator means "losing face". This is a very interesting aspect of position negotiation.

Position negotiation is more frequently used and requires less work: it is also less effective than interest-based negotiation. Position negotiation in a non-cooperative game is conducive to Nash Equilibrium. The stability of a compromise does not guarantee the optimal outcome to either party. Therefore, the evolution of negotiation theory for treating non-cooperative games is a very interesting tool which could find application in healthcare management.

The Harvard Negotiation Project (HNP) was developed to study alternatives to position negotiation. The objective was to find new models of negotiation given the obvious limitations of position negotiation. The HNP determined that behind the position in a negotiation were interests. The position was simply one of a number of possible quantifications of an interest. One example might be a teenager who wishes to stay out late with friends and a parent who does not want her child to stay out after 12.30 am. The interests of the parent generally regard the perceived safety of the child: drinking and driving, etc. The interests of the child are wanting to stay out with their peers. Behind the two positions: "I want to to stay out until 3", and "you cannot stay out past 12.30 am", are interests which can be met by finding alternative solutions to arguing about what time to come home. However, if each party states his/her position, it becomes difficult to speak about interests because if the parent lets the child come home at 3, the parent has "lost face". Vice versa, the stability of an agreement based on the hour the child should come home is weak, as the child's friends go home at 3 am.

The study of position negotiation demonstrated a psychological facet of position negotiation. The person and the problem were intertwined. If a parent told the child 12.30 am, conceding all ground and letting the child stay out until 3 am was a "loss of face". The face of the person is connected to his/her position and vice versa. One of the interesting developments of this theory was the idea of separating the person from the problem by exploring the interests of each person before identifying a position, or a solution to the problem.

This work developed a theory of interest-based negotiation. The HNP identified some fundamental rules for avoiding position-based negotiation and focusing on interest-based negotiation.

Separate the person from the problem. It is possible to be attentive to the person and to the relationship, and tough with the problem.

Identify interests. Interests inform positions. Positions are solutions, while interests are the why behind the position.

Measure a good agreement with process not with trust. A good agreement focuses on rewarding reliability. In a hospital budget negotiation measuring reduced length of stay may mean producing multiple admissions for a single health problem. The process is not being measured. The system is trusting the actors to act in cooperative agreements, however the measurement system is not well defined, it appears to be based on trust.

The following example illustrates the potential for application of interest-based negotiation to conflicts and managerial problems that are present in the healthcare system.

Antonio was the CEO of an important research firm. He retired when he was 60 and continued to pursue his scientific interests: reading the latest issues of *Science* and other scientific publications. He and his wife loved spending time in the mountains, hiking and finding mushrooms. When he was 64 he became a bit confused. Numbers confused him. On his wife and two daughters' suggestion he underwent neurological tests. One of these tests was to take nine away from 100 and keep going until he got as close to 0 as possible. He arrived to 91 and was unable to proceed; however, he was fully aware that he used to know how to do this. The tests found neurological dysfunction but were inconclusive. The testing experience had been so humiliating, that he refused to undergo further analysis. He was aware of his progressive confusion and hated it. He was still able to function in most family activities, to read, watch movies and recognize people. He was then diagnosed with cancer. Both the operation and the chemotherapy put him in the unfamiliar environment of the hospital. His confusion increased dramatically. Since his first operation he is no longer able to read or follow a TV show. By his bedside there are no more books.

His wife continues to ask the oncologist when she can plan to go to the mountains. The oncologist is annoyed because this search for a time table is not consonant with the cure which requires successive evaluations and decisions.

> In private, the wife is very upset because while he may be cured of his cancer, his mental state is regressing at an incredible pace. While she has no scientific evidence that the two situations are connected, the relationship with the oncologist is deteriorating and she feels intimidated asking for an interest-based negotiation and the intervention of a neurologist. The oncologist is fighting the cancer, however his wife is fighting to go to the mountains. The oncologist continues to see the issue of the tumor and recently prescribed a fourth session of chemotherapy which eliminated the possibility for them to pass some of the summer in the mountains.

The question here is: is this case being managed?

This case is evidence of a conflict and a position-based negotiation. Interest-based negotiation would reveal that as things stand: the person is being confused with the problem, positions prevail while interests are going unmet, no process outcomes have been negotiated and the future family-physician relationship is being damaged.

The oncologist has identified a tumor and his position is to do everything within his specialization to cure his patient of the cancer. The wife has identified a quality of life issue and is doing everything within her power to take her husband to the mountains.

The people are confused with the problem. The oncologist has identified the wife as a trouble maker. The wife has identified the oncologist as responsible for the rapidly progressing neurological damage in her husband.

The larger interests of the case have not been addressed. Have all the professional roles (oncologist, neurologist, GP, family and patient) built a blended relationship to manage Antonio's case?

Furthermore, there is no common definition of a positive outcome of the cure process. While no more cancer may be an optimal outcome from the oncologist's perspective, in the absence of more information it may be attributed a negative value from the patient's family's perspective.

Lastly, the relationship between the oncologist and the wife is progressively deteriorating.

Interest-based negotiation is missing. There is no larger lens within which to examine the interests of the parties, the missing information (is the chemotherapy worsening the neurological conditions of the patient?) and the possibility of more than one possible solution. Regardless of the patient's cancer outcome, the case is not being managed.

Negotiation theory enables a reading of this case that shows that "no more cancer" is not a measure of outcome for the family until their interests and the missing information have been considered.

In the simplest scenario, this interest-based negotiation would simply determine that "no more cancer" is a suitable outcome measure for both parties. This would eliminate the conflict and develop the relationship between the family and the hospital. In a more complex scenario the missing information could entail redefining the objectives of care, and the role of the actors. One example of a possible redefinition might be that the oncologist is directed towards providing palliative care.

The interest-based negotiation approach to the situation helps identify the lack of a managerial response to the situation. The situation goes unmanaged rather than being mismanaged. The theory of interest-based negotiation can be a helpful tool in identifying the content of the managerial function for the healthcare professional in the healthcare system.

Post-Nash developments

Subsequent work by economists after the Nash theories were concerned with the implications of Nash's findings. They reasoned that Nash had discovered that optimal outcomes and stability often did not coincide in a non-cooperative game. If the parties pursued stability they achieved suboptimal outcomes. If they achieved optimal outcomes, these were unstable over time. This was not a pretty picture of non-cooperative transactions.

The hypothesis that they pursued was that it was possible to create a series of conditions in a non-cooperative game that allowed the optimal outcome to become stable. They worked and experimented with the prisoner's dilemma and other non-cooperative games to figure out the outside conditions which could make an optimal solution appear stable to the parties in a non-cooperative game. In simple terms they asked themselves under what conditions can we make a non-cooperative game function like a cooperative game without resorting to the third party as guarantor?

Unlike negotiation theory, which identified strengthening or at worst not weakening the relationship between negotiators as one of the interests of the parties in a negotiation process, the economists worked on identifying the threats to the relationship between negotiators and how these could impact non-collaborative games and Nash equilibrium.

The two economists who pursued post-Nash theories were Harsanyi and Selten. They identified scenarios that would modify the equilibrium point of non-cooperative games like the prisoner's dilemma from an unfavourable to an optimal outcome. They were interested in what needed to happen in the non-cooperative game in order for stability and positive outcome to coincide.

They identified two conditions in which the equilibrium point and the optimal outcome would coincide in a non-cooperative game: a long time frame and a threat to the relationship between the negotiating parties. A "real threat" to a long term relationship between the negotiating parties would bring equilibrium to an optimal outcome. One of the players had to threaten not to cooperate ever again if the other party defected from the agreement. The disincentive to non-cooperate would strengthen the incentive to cooperate.[64] The incentive to cooperate was built on the risk of not cooperating, rather than on assigning a positive value to the relationship. This is called "non-cooperative collusion".[65] Non-cooperative collusion could in fact stabilize the system at a positive outcome. However, non-cooperative collusion was observed in the long term nature of the relationship.

Negotiation theory takes the long term relationship and makes the same argument. Instead of building on the threat of abandoning a relationship forever, negotiation theory identifies the necessity to build relationships and negotiate at the same time. Negotiation theory argues that every negotiator has an interest in finding an agreement and in preserving the relationship. The economists also argue that there needs to be a strong incentive to build the relationship (given by the indefinite time span in which the relationship is going to take place) and consequently, the cooperative and most positive outcome can be achieved. The premise of negotiation theory is not based on disincentives, but on incentives to build the relationship and to come to a "fair" agreement.

The other modifications to the Nash equilibrium were called "subgames". During a game between two players it was not reasonable to assume that each player would act only rationally, but would also make mistakes.[66] In studying actual dilemmas, it was discovered that players threaten "improbable consequences" of non-cooperation of the other player. This is called the "trembling hand" approach to negotiation. If the threat is taken seriously, the negotiator achieves the best possible outcome, if the threat is not taken seriously, the negotiator's outcome will not be optimal. There are small probabilities that the threat will not be taken seriously however, in the event that the other player makes "a mistake", threatening a behaviour that will not generate "an optimal outcome" contrasts Nash equilibrium.

In conclusion, the specific nature of the healthcare context, both in interdepartment relations within a hospital, relations between primary care centres and hospitals, relationships between primary care centres and general practitioners, and relationships among GPs, may be managed more effectively with an attention to the non-collaborative nature of these relationships. By identifying the non-cooperative nature of the organization, management action can encourage self-enforcing cooperation between parties. Negotiation theory can be an important tool in identifying common interests and facilitating self-enforcing cooperation. Post-Nash theory on indefinite relationships and "trembling hand" might be additional tools with which to produce alternative equilibrium and optimal outcomes in health system management.

4

Trust and Rational Choice

Introduction to trust and rational choice

The previous chapters – on person-role blended relationship, the doctor-patient relationship, and healthcare management as a non-cooperative game – have identified the specific nature of healthcare management and the importance of communication theory, negotiation and cooperation among professionals, patients and their families. Another way of looking at these themes, in order to shed new light on healthcare management is to consider the importance of trust and rational choice.

Trust is an expectation that the promise of another individual or group can be depended upon.[67] Studies of trust indicate that people need to trust when they are in a situation where they perceive risk. Risk is determined by the possibility that the other party will exploit vulnerability. The trustee is the person in whom trust is placed. The risk is that the trustee, instead of assuming the responsibility for the trust that has been placed with him/her, will take advantage of the vulnerability that has been exposed.

Situations which require trust are uncertain and therefore their outcomes depend on having placed trust in a trustworthy individual or organization. When an individual trusts someone, the individual hopes to have made a good choice. Hope is defined as: "to cherish a desire with the expectation or belief of fulfillment"[68] and trust places this expectation into someone else's hands. So trust and hope are both born from uncertainty and the lack of control over outcomes.[69] When people lose their health, they put trust in their physicians and healthcare processes and hope that they will get better again.

Trust has more than just a relationship dimension: it is also based on rational judgment.[70,71] An individual does not place trust in someone just because he/she declares that he/she will do something. Many realms are evaluated: the intentions of the trustee (as far as they are known) the options the trustee has and their consequences, and the trustee's competence and ability to do something. By placing trust in someone else, the individual makes a prediction that the trustee will do what they promise in the future. The interesting thing about trust is that the individual has to place trust in the trustee before evaluating if their trust is well placed. Trust is forward looking, but in placing it, the credibility of the trustee has to be evaluated.

The word trust has many uses but all evoke the forward looking nature of the transaction. "I trust that you are well" means "I hope that you are well."[72] In its business application, a "trust" represents the decision on the part of property owners to have their properties administered by others for their benefit, in the future.

The objective when one is uncertain and vulnerable and looking for an individual or an organization in which to place trust, is to avoid a trusting relationship with someone who would intentionally betray that trust. This attempt to calculate a reasonable risk when placing trust is known in the literature as rational choice.

Naturally, rational choice plays a role in who is best qualified to care for my interests, whether these be my children, my reputation or my property. The same goes for healthcare. Part of the trust in a healthcare facility is based on a rational choice.

The first part of this chapter will explore trust and the second part will balance the theory of trust with some rational tools that are important for evaluating the person that is going to be entrusted. The point being that in a situation of uncertainty and risk, the mere declaration of trustworthiness is simply not strong enough to justify an act of trust. We use more rational tools to back up a "trust me" from another person or organization and rarely or only in situations where there appear to be no alternatives is a "trust me" alone enough of a guarantee to trust. When a patient gets very sick, the patient and the family will almost always get a second opinion. The affirmations of the first person they turn to are not going to be enough for them to entrust the health of a loved one. More than just the feeling of trust will inform the decision to trust. Rational considerations will inform the decision to trust also.

The healthcare organization is an organization that must by definition wrestle with risk and uncertainty. In this chapter, trust and rational choice will be explored as a potential organizational paradigm with which to approach healthcare management.

Trust and loss of trust in the healthcare organization: interpersonal and organizational

Healthcare organizations look like non-cooperative games. This means that when the organization is certain and in control (Nash equilibrium) it cannot achieve optimal outcomes. In order for the organization to achieve optimal outcomes it must undertake risk and uncertainty. Optimal outcomes are not stable ones, so risk is an intrinsic part of the structure of the relationships within and among healthcare organizations. A critical component therefore in cementing the organization and in building a management paradigm for healthcare is trust.

Trust exists on two levels, interpersonal and organizational. The doctor-patient relationship is founded on interpersonal trust, however the organization lives the consequences, both positive and negative, of the interpersonal trust relationship. Likewise, the trust relationship among members of the healthcare organization influences the inter-personal trust relationship between physicians and patients.

One example of how trust between members of the organization influences trust levels between the physician and the patient is given by a mother who gave birth to her first child, born at 4.4 kilos. Due to the size of the baby, she endured 16 hours of labour and then suffered a post-natal hemorrhage.

Anna and her newborn son were hospitalized for ten days. In the hospital, mothers were invited to seminars by a dietician who taught them about the correct diet for breastfeeding mothers. The dietician emphasized the importance of not trying to lose weight while breast-feeding and of avoiding certain foods which would significantly alter the taste of the milk. Among the foods to be avoided were: cauliflower, onion, hot pepper, and garlic. Anna was impressed with the dietician's simple explanations and guidelines. She was also very nervous because she had lost her self-confidence with the post-natal hemorrhage and became skeptical about her capabilities to undertake natural breast-feeding. Furthermore, though her baby was very robust, he had been losing weight because her breastfeeding had not yet produced any milk. The nurses reassured her that this was normal, but she remained dubious and uncertain. That evening her dinner was served: spaghetti with cauliflower. Cauliflower was a forbidden ingredient, and dieting was forbidden as well. The mother's trust in the hospital and in the dietician dropped dramatically, as she realized that the dietician had no relationship with the kitchen and vice versa.

This case shows that lack of trust within the organization will affect patient trust in specific interpersonal relationships, and it shows that the organizational paradigm actually forced the patient into non-compliance. If she ate the spaghetti, she ate a forbidden ingredient, if she didn't eat, she reduced her calorie intake.

Healthcare organizations, unlike other organizations are filled with uncertainty. Uncertainty as to the best treatment paths, uncertainty as to the outcomes of its efforts, uncertainty concerning how the patient will behave.

In other organizations, where there is more certainty, there is no need to act on the basis of trust. In fact, it is possible in certain areas to eliminate or account for risk and to put mechanisms into place that put relationships into an area of certainty. "Trust cannot exist in an environment of certainty; if it did, it would do so trivially".[73]

Cooperation is to be distinguished from trust. If the organization eliminates risks and uncertainties, it is possible to cooperate without trusting. In fact, Nash defined a cooperative game as one in which a third party guaranteed that cooperation would take place. An example of how the third party takes trust out of the act of cooperation may be exemplified with the honour code in certain North American Universities: students must sign an agreement with the institution stating they will not cheat and if caught will be expelled. When the student signs the honour code, cheating is not about trusting your colleagues anymore, it is about breaking a rule, and has consequences.

The healthcare organization in contrast, is filled with risk and uncertainty. In order to achieve cooperation without a third party, the organization must work with a model of trust. In the healthcare organization when members of the organization lack trust, there are various indicators of trust dysfunction: doctor-shopping by patients, non-compliance, malpractice suits, risk management issues and physician absenteeism are just some examples. The specificity of healthcare management is that it also depends on trust to build teams and cooperation within the organization. Trust is an important component in a range of organizational activities, such as teamwork, leadership, goal setting and negotiation.[74] Research has shown that poor teamwork is more connected to physician absenteeism for sickness than other causes like work overload and low job control.[75] Therefore interpersonal and organizational trust are intertwined.

By examining the principle of inadvertent marketing, it is possible to conclude that trust must be present within the healthcare organization in order to effectively support the existing trust between physician and patient. Various critical issues in healthcare management today can be viewed as stemming from lack of trust. Clinical error management models and malpractice suits are evidence that betrayal of trust is a recognized problem in the organization. Dr. Berwick, founder of the Institute for Healthcare Improvement (IHI), studied six types of secondary hospital-based infections, like hospital-acquired pneumonia, for example, all of which can be clinically prevented. According to IHI statistics, these avoidable secondary infections cause 230 unnecessary deaths a year in any given 500-bed hospital. If each hospital were to correctly apply these existing guidelines, a conservative hypothesis is that death could be avoided in 125 of every 230 cases. Over the entire system and total number of beds in the United States, this amounts to a concrete possibility of preventing 100,000 unnecessary deaths a year.[76]

Medical malpractice and secondary hospital-based infections are huge problems not because of a lack of knowledge as to what should have been done; the Acute Myocardial Infarction (AMI) guidelines exist and are effective if applied, as are some basic rules of communication. These problems are difficult to tackle, not because there are no known solutions to them, but because they are generated from the emotional context of error.[77] The emotional context of error is characterized by anger, blame, and fear of errors. When people in organizations are afraid of the consequences of their mistakes they will tend to hide these.

A fascinating case of fear of making mistakes can be found reading the report of the commission that investigated the US space shuttle Columbia explosion. The recommendations of the senate investigation committee that looked into the tragedy, argue in an entire chapter that the space shuttle accident was completely preventable, from a technical perspective. There was the knowledge and the technology to solve the problems before the accident happened, just like the application of AMI guidelines can do the same. However, the culture of fear of error and consequent habit of the organization to hide problems, were so enormous that they caused the accident as much as the technical error that was identified.[78]

Loss of trust is a critical cause of organizational dysfunction. Betrayal of trust is defined as a conscious decision and is based on the same considerations seen in the non-cooperative game: "Betrayal is one of the options in the decision process where the most attractive of two or more options is chosen and the attractiveness of the betrayal option is a function of a critical assessment of the overall situation as perceived by the trustee".[79] In applying clinical risk management principles, one of the critical issues is that staff have to trust the organization. They have to trust that there will be no negative consequences attached to reporting their own and the errors of others.[80]

At issue here is trust and how knowledge is managed. It has been observed in macroeconomics that high trust societies possess a competitive advantage. Knowledge is shared and litigation costs are limited.[81] The data on litigation costs in healthcare indicate that the healthcare organization is a low-trust organization; 10% of healthcare costs in the United States are malpractice costs, and another 8% are the costs of undeclared and unrecognized functional illiteracy, for a total of US $180 billion a year. When a patient does not declare to his/her physician that there is a literacy problem, the patient does not trust the physician with this sensitive and critical information. "Patients and physicians…live and interact in a culture characterized by anger, blame, guilt, fear, frustration and distrust regarding healthcare errors. The public has responded by escalating the punishment for error. Clinicians and some healthcare organizations generally have responded by suppression, stonewalling and cover up".[82]

There are many reasons to critically examine this low trust environment in healthcare. It has many hidden costs besides those that have been monetarily quantified. In the realm of patient care, management of chronic disease has seen the growing role of patient participation in healthcare management. Self-care practices abound. Some examples include lifestyle and diet of the patient in managing obesity, diabetes and hypertension. Patient compliance and the lack of doctor-shopping has been connected to patient trust in the physician. Today chronic patient non-compliance is estimated at 50% through all age groups and illnesses. This causes the health status of the patient to worsen faster and therefore, become extremely costly to manage, though the exact estimation of the consequent costs of this has not been quantified.

Building organizational trust in healthcare management

Trust then is a very important tool in healthcare management. It is considered to have an indirect influence on adherence to therapy, continuity of a patient with a provider, and encourages the patient to participate actively in the care and diagnosis process.[83] "Trust is forward-looking and reflects a commitment to an ongoing relationship, whereas satisfaction tends to be based on past experience and refers to an assessment of provider's performance. It has been suggested that trust is a more sensitive indicator of performance than patient satisfaction".[84] In the general literature, patients have a high level of trust in their physicians and nurses and a low level of trust in the organization and the system. This was confirmed in a study of 2,777 British patients: patients largely trusted their physicians. 83% of patients trusted that their physicians were educated, trained, and the best in the world. 68% trusted that doctors provided them with good guidance and took them seriously. However, on a health system level, only 38% of patients trusted that medical care would not be compromised by the shortening of waiting lists. Only 30% trusted that patients would not be victims of costs of care, and only 32% trusted that cost cutting did not disadvantage patients. On an organizational level only 53% of patients believed that healthcare providers cooperate effectively and only 48% believed that they would not receive conflicting information.[85]

This general finding of high physician-patient trust, extremely low public trust and mediocre organizational trust has also been found in the Dutch healthcare system.[86]

In the public healthcare system, chronic patients are managed by a team of doctors, rather than by a single physician. Therefore, interpersonal trust needs to be extensive and part of the trust paradigm needs to be present in the relationships among members of the organization. From patient care, to the relationship between professionals, trust is a critical issue for the reputation of the organization and of its members.

In healthcare, a specific factor in building organizational trust is the issue of patient anxiety. Patients inevitably experience anxiety about their health, however the organizational context can increase patient anxiety and consequently reduce patient trust. In a recent study of organizational and interpersonal trust in the Oncology Division at Niguarda Hospital in Milan, various "patient anxiety issues" were discussed and their effect on the organization and patient health were analysed. The following case study shows how trust can be studied and used to improve performance in the organization.

At Niguarda Hospital in the Oncology Division, interpersonal trust is extremely well-developed. A patient describing her first hospital day describes the following episode "I was greeted by a nurse who had never seen me before, however she said to me 'You are the woman who called on Thursday, I was the one who spoke to you over the phone'". Interpersonal trust in this hospital is extremely high, patients in fact have a high level of trust not only in their physician of choice but also in the equipe of physicians and nurses that assist them. However, the trust is born in the interpersonal relationship style of the Division. The trust in the process, the organization of care, and in self-care abilities are obscured by the importance of the relationship with the professional staff. In the absence of a professional figure, patients become extremely anxious. This happens both at home and in the hospital.

Trust is present when the patient has a personal contact. Every attempt to depersonalize information and its delivery while developing patient trust is ineffective. Patient anxiety reduces the patient's ability to read and assimilate written information of any kind, from informational brochures, to the next appointment, to the letter of discharge or the results of diagnostic exams. Patients describe their anxiety about symptoms that they have at home "I spend hours reading and rereading the same paragraph trying to understand if what I feel is normal". The head nurse described phone calls to patients who failed to show up for scheduled hospital admission "But nobody told me that I had to be rehospitalized. I did not read the letter of discharge!".

When the patient experiences anxiety, he/she is no longer able to trust the process or take responsibility for self-care. Patient anxiety is therefore a critical symptom of distrust in the organization, and its antecedent management is important in building the reputation of the hospital itself.

The chief physician of oncology and the head nurse, together with other members of the professional team, worked together with patients and families to identify when patient anxiety set in. Four moments were identified: waiting rooms, written material unaccompanied by oral communication, organizing follow-up appointments, and physicians and nurses being stopped in informal settings like corridors and waiting rooms for quick consultations.

One oncology patient in an interview about waiting rooms for chemotherapy declared "in the waiting room patients exchange horror stories, stories of undefinable aches and pains of all kinds including toothaches and attribute all of these to chemotherapy. So much so, that whatever discomfort I feel when I get home, I attribute to chemotherapy, even the fact that the television doesn't work!!". In a study funded by the Region of Lombardy, Niguarda Hospital decided to work on reducing patient anxiety.

In Niguarda Hospital, waiting rooms created anxiety. While there are scheduled appointments, the hospital is well-known as the best emergency hospital in Milan. Therefore, everything from a visit with a specialist, to a diagnostic exam can be late due to an emergency. To make matters more complicated, oncology patients regularly show up two hours early for their appointments. They do this because they are anxious about being late, and at the same time are anxious to get the results of their health status. Though the organization has done everything to discourage this behaviour, patients continue to come early to appointments. This means that waiting rooms are a place where both for organizational reasons and patient choice, patients spend a great deal of time without a professional.

Waiting rooms are fertile ground for raising patient anxiety as patients discuss their health stories with each other. Even when patients are given appointment times that are respected by the organization, the waiting room is still a place where patients meet and raise each other's anxiety level. If the layout of the hospital is such that physicians' paths cross the patients, patients will inevitably ask a "quick question" to their trusted physician. Physicians often do not know offhand the specifics of the situation and by their own admission are often unable to give informed responses. Oncology patients at the hospital are managed by a team of oncologists. This means that the patient will be given the next available appointment rather than be guaranteed an appointment with a preferred oncologist. When anxiety in the patient mounts, the patient will go to the scheduled appointment but also informally seek out the "interpersonal" trusted physician for a second informal consultation.

Furthermore, regularly scheduled ambulatory check-up visits often require consultations with other specialists or diagnostic exams within a short period to determine whether the medication is causing harmful side effects. This is a problem similar to the triage problem. It is not an emergency but it cannot wait for the "regular" appointment. In this case, oncologists must get on the phone and negotiate a spare moment in the next ten days where their patients can be received. The patient therefore leaves the hospital knowing he/she has to do follow-up quickly but without an appointment. There are huge costs: in time for physicians and in anxiety for patients.

Patient anxiety in oncology mounts when retrieving diagnostic exams. In Italy, diagnostic exams for reasons of privacy are picked up by patients themselves. In order to make sure that the patient has had time to undergo diagnostic testing and to retrieve the exam, appointments with the oncologist are scheduled at a safe distance from the date of the diagnostic examination. Some patients are so anxious, they keep their results in a sealed envelope and ask their physician to open the envelope. Others open them, and do not know how to interpret the information. They then wait ten days for their appointment with mounting panic.

When the patient believes he or she has experienced a relapse, doctor-shopping, alternative medicine and other signs of lack of trust set in.[87] When patients stop trusting their physician, they often do not tell their physician this is taking place. In Italy, for example, a study of the Ministry of Health showed that 10–60% of oncology patients turn to alternative medicine. Of this group, 47% turn to figures recommended by a non-physician. Furthermore, 63% of patients who do turn to alternative treatments, do not inform their oncologists. This certainly can undermine everything, from the perceived efficacy of treatment to compliance and other health-related issues.

Managing patient anxiety in oncology strengthens the organization and organizational trust. Niguarda Hospital decided to invest in building organizational trust to reduce patient anxiety.

Volunteers have been assigned to waiting rooms in emergency medicine and day hospital waiting rooms. Their role is to manage patient anxiety by helping patients to understand the organization of care and to manage the experience sharing that goes on in waiting rooms. The volunteers are trained specifically by physicians and nurses.

Furthermore, new technology allows exam results to be read electronically by the physician. One novelty in the Niguarda Hospital Oncology process is to schedule the appointment with the physician first and have the patient learn about diagnostic results directly from the physician. Only after this does the patient collect exam results so that the patient never holds an unexplained result.

Weekly scheduled consultation hours with the most frequently requested specialists have been organized so that patients can be told immediately that the cardiologist will be seeing oncology patients Wednesday from 10–12.

Lastly, in building the new hospital, waiting rooms will be designed so that staff and patients move in separate spaces so that anxious patients do not see professional staff walking by and stop them in the corridors.

As can be seen through this case, patient-physician trust is high, while trust in the system is very low, and organizational trust is also compromised. The importance of low levels of public trust in the system have a negative consequence on the physician-patient relationship: "Patients will more often ask for a second opinion: they will obtain services from 'alternative' practitioners...Another possible consequence of a lack of trust could be a lower level of compliance with therapy".[88] As is evident in the Niguarda study, it is possible to make small changes in order to increase organizational trust. These changes are not costly and can reduce costs, however they do require the organization to design service delivery to increase patient trust in the organization and decrease patient anxiety.

Components of trust: rational choice

As mentioned in the introduction to this chapter, trust alone is not sufficient to protect a person, or an organization from the uncertainty and risk that the act of trust involves in the first place. Beyond the trust placed in the individual or institution, there is some due diligence that comes with trusting an individual or an organization. This rational part of the trust process is very important because if it is well understood it is a risk management tool in the act of trusting.

As explained in the examples, the lack of trust between members of the organization will influence the patient's trust in the physician and in the organization. The case seen earlier in this chapter of the breast-feeding mother in a dilemma: looking at the spaghetti with cauliflower that she is not supposed to eat, while knowing she is not supposed to diet either, is a case in point of how trust follows inadvertent marketing principles. The case exemplifies how her trust in the dietician plummets when she realizes that the dietician is not coordinated with the menu planner in the kitchen of the hospital. There is no third party guaranteeing that the dietary consultant to the mothers on the maternity floor is cooperating with the menu planner in the kitchen. The operation depends on peer to peer collaboration in the non-cooperative game.

The healthcare organization, as this case demonstrates, depends on peer to peer cooperation in the absence of a third party as a guarantor. The healthcare organization cannot reduce risk and uncertainty so that trust becomes a trivial aspect of cooperation. The healthcare organization requires trust exactly because it is an organization characterized by risk and uncertainty. However, in order to run a trusting organization it is important that its members are familiar with the tools of rational choice, because it is a common language that can be used to reduce risk and uncertainty. Rational choice is a risk management tool for peers to use in developing blended relationships with one another in the organization. "Trust me" is never reason enough to trust another person, department or organization. Rational choice together with trust can better serve the healthcare organization's cultural paradigm.

Theories of rational choice have two dimensions that interact with one another: descriptive theories describe the actual behaviour of individuals or systems, and prescriptive theories prescribe optimal behaviour. In short, the prescriptive theories develop rational tools for making better choices and the descriptive or behavioural theories try to understand why nobody uses them. An example of the dialogue between prescriptive theory and behavioural theory in healthcare can be seen in the development of a prescriptive tool such as economic evaluation. Economic evaluation carefully weighs multiple variables (clinical, economic and quality of life) to identify alternative care paths and direct clinicians to those which are optimal. Economic evaluation is prescriptive. Decision makers and their behaviour is what behavioural theory studies. It is interesting to note that economic evaluation does not inform the decision making process for decision makers. In fact, while evidence-based studies are constructed rationally and make informed arguments they are not "trusted" by decision makers. In fact, it would seem that the capacity to make good decisions diminishes with the increased number of rational choices. One of the critical issues in economic evaluation is that even when decision makers have read the information provided by the theory, this information does not influence decisions. Theorists who develop prescriptive models try to adapt these models to make them useful tools.[89]

Behavioural models, such as that of bounded rationality suggest that it is too costly to identify all the elements needed to inform rational choices and that people tend to behave by bounding the field from which they draw elements to make a decision.[90] Bounded rationality in healthcare has often produced Kafkaesque, or absurd, results. In a case of the Local Health Authority in the Emilia Region of Italy this can be observed clearly.

Pap test screening at the Local Health Authority of **XXX** was well developed. At a certain point, the services underwent a quality accreditation and cost saving process. In this process, it was discovered that mailing pap test results one at a time cost significantly more than accumulating results and doing a bulk mailing. Therefore the cost saving group decided on a bulk mail response. However, in the new process no one thought to distinguish the mail process on the basis of whether the exam had a positive or negative result. Therefore positive results for pap tests were kept along with negative ones until a sufficient number of envelopes had accumulated. The purpose of the screening itself had been thwarted by the mailing room!

This is an example of the limits of bounded rationality, in that by limiting the size of the problem being examined, there are limits to the vision of its solution, in this case the result is both absurd and painful. The cost savings team bounded the field to costs and no longer considered the clinical significance of the information that was being sent.

Expected utility, rational choice and patterns of irrational choice

Rational choice is a tool in moments of uncertainty and any moment that requires trust, is by definition, uncertain. A US General, active in the Vietnam war, and brought out of retirement by the Pentagon to test new war strategies, General Van Riper said "say you are looking at a chess board. Is there anything you can't see? No. But are you guaranteed to win? Not at all, because you can't see what the other guy is thinking".[91] The basic mathematical premise of prescriptive rationality proposed by Von Neumann and Morgenstern stated that people make decisions to maximize expected utility. The theoretical definition they proposed of expected utility was personal value, so personal value is a broad concept and not to be confused with a simple monetary gain. Expected utility is what the decision maker wishes to satisfy. It is a concept which has three rational premises: the consideration of all alternative courses of action in terms of their possible consequences, the probability of these consequences, and the assessment of the alternatives within the rules of probability. Personal value variables are weighted numerically and through this rational calculation, the best decision is identified.

Behavioural economists and psychologists on the other hand reach a different conclusion in asking themselves how decision makers, whether they be individuals, groups, organizations, or governments actually choose. Their observations indicate that decision making is often totally irrational and systematically so. Patterns of irrationality have been observed. Some examples of these patterns include sunken costs, applying probability to the past, budgeting, framing, representative thinking, memory and imagination, learning from experience, hindsight bias, anchoring, the compound probability fallacy and many others. Some of these examples will be illustrated, as all of them share two characteristics, lack of knowledge of probability theory and the "hubris" of human intuitive judgement, that makes people believe that the mysteries of the human mind explain the unexplainable.

The compound probability fallacy depends on "seeing" the future and imaging that a series of independent events are more, rather than less, likely to occur together. According to probability, the likelihood two independent events occuring together is much less than the likelihood of one event occurring. This probability fallacy occurred systematically in Local Health Authorities (LHAs) in Italy where prevention, increasing homecare and diminishing hospitalization is a key objective of LHAs. The following two examples illustrate the compound probability fallacy.

> Managing low level clinical needs at home was functioning well in LHAs. Placing a GP, a nurse, and a social worker in people's homes for a number of hours a week proved effective in reducing unnecessary emergency room visits and hospitalizations in chronic patients. The assumption was that this model could be extended to patients with more severe health problems by adding specialists to the group visiting patients at home. Services were designed for respiratory problems and an ambulance with artificial ventilation equipment was dedicated to homecare services. No patients agreed to participate in the initiative. What is the probability that someone who could not breathe would also be at home?

Another issue that has encountered the compound probability fallacy is domestic violence.

> In a local authority in the Piedmont Region, there were a significant number of cases of domestic violence correlated with consequent health risks for women. The Local Authority organized all the organizations which may have seen, from their perspective, domestic violence. Among these were the LHA, the local hospital and the police department and collectively they invested 600,000 Euros to open a "window" service to battered women. Resources were invested in training, finding spaces in different parts of the area and staffing these windows. At the end of 18 months, not a single battered woman had turned to the service for assistance. What is the probability that someone who is beaten at home would also be seen in front of a window for battered women?

Sunken costs are investments that were made in the past. Rationally, they should not affect future decisions. For example, if you have already made a non-refundable 200 Euro deposit for a vacation, and you decide that you would rather stay home, the decision to go on vacation to honour the sunken cost goes against where you want to be. Your assets have decreased by 200 Euros but that has already happened regardless of whether you go on vacation or stay home. The same goes for a patient choosing a course of therapy. A specialist might charge 200 Euros for a visit and suggest a care process. If the patient is not convinced, the specialist visit is a sunken cost. Continuing to follow the course of therapy, without believing in it because 200 Euros have already been invested, may account for some compliance problems. Rationally, sunken costs should not affect decisions about the future.[92]

Another pattern of irrational behaviour is applying probability to the past rather than to the future. Probability examines the possibility of one event occurring on the next occasion.

If I throw a coin and I get three heads in a row, it would not be a correct application of probability to count the three heads in determining the fourth toss. It would lead me to believe that I had a higher probability of tossing a tail than a head. Each toss has a 50-50 chance of turning up heads.[93]

If a couple has had seven boys, the probability of conceiving seven boys is one divided by two to the seventh or 1/128, but the probability that the eighth child is a girl is exactly 50-50. Just like the probability of getting tails on the fourth toss is not at all influenced by the previous three.[94]

This is the basis of rational decision making.

Budgeting is another example. Budgeting sets out sums of resources for various aspects of an organization or a family. Let's imagine a family budget.

The amount allotted for a car will be superior to the amount allotted for family entertainment. However, when the car dealer offers a low-fidelity stereo system in the car for 500 Euros more, this is not weighted against the family entertainment budget, but seen as a relatively small increment compared to the car budget. Would you spend 500 Euros out of the entertainment budget for a low-fidelity stereo? No. Would you spend it out of the car budget? Yes.[95]

The rational choice view of managing assets suggests that before being allocated they need to be considered in their totality.

Representative thinking is another fallacy.

If a psychologist who works with child abusers, asserts that a child abuser will always repeat his/her behaviour, the psychologist actually knows that child abusers who seek therapy repeat their behaviour. The psychologist does not know anything about child abusers who do not seek therapy.[96]

What to do about these biases? In part they are fallacies based on an incomplete or fallacious understanding of probability. In part we are overly conditioned by experience in choosing our representative sample. We do not realize how necessary it is to take precautions against ourselves. Odysseus can teach an interesting lesson with regards to guarding ourselves against human hubris.

> The sirens were nymphs in Greek mythology. They were depicted with the head of a woman and the body of a bird and inhabited an island in the midst of dangerous rocks for seafarers. Their singing was so engaging that anyone who heard them was drawn to them and would consequently be shipwrecked on the rocks. Odysseus escaped them by tying himself to the mast of his ship and plugging the ears of his sailors.

The metaphor of the sirens illustrates that human hubris must be figuratively "tied to the mast" to guarantee the ability to make rational choices. The belief that people make better choices without using rational judgement (the sirens do not apply here) has been proven false again and again. It is important to tie up the instinct that leads people to ignore the steps necessary in making rational choices.

The decision analysis model proposed by Morgenstern and Neumann is generally considered "inhuman" because it does work with numerical values, even if these are only a representation of personal values. "Research indicates that numbers in a linear model can be well used in making predictions. The implication that they can serve well also in choice and preference contexts is immediate. Using them however, requires us to overcome a view (not supported by the research) that the 'mysteries of the human mind' allow us to reach superior conclusions without their aid".[97]

When examining trust and rational choice the issues at hand are complex, decision makers do not "trust" predictive models, and yet, these are always more reliable than intuitive alternatives:[98] human beings must try to face necessary uncertainty by making decisions that make sense. The need for rational choice concerns patients trusting their physicians, physicians trusting each other, and the management system in general. Trust and rational choice are connected. In making a decision to trust a person or an organization, often rational choice models are used to evaluate and choose the trustee.

The debate: rational choice and intuitive management

The Nobel prize winning poet, Joseph Brodsky, in a book of essays entitled "On Grief and Reason" identifies an important issue that aids us in understanding the negative connotations that rational choice theory has undeservedly called to itself. Though he is discussing history and historians, he clearly identifies a perceived distinguishing characteristic between rational choice theory and the "mysteries of the human mind" today known as intuitive management. In speaking about historians, he says "Objectivity, of course, is the motto of every historian, and that's why passion is normally ruled out – since as the saying goes, it blinds. One wonders, however, whether a passionate response, in such a context, wouldn't amount to a greater human objectivity, for disembodied intelligence carries no weight... In other words, the quest for objectivity of interpretation takes precedence over the sentiments caused by what is interpreted. One wonders, then what is the significance of interpretation: Is history simply an instrument for measuring how far we can remove ourselves from events, a sort of anti-thermometer?"[99]

Intuitive management develops rational choice and adds non-verbal information to the analysis: specifically, facial expression, tone of voice, and body language. Intuitive management considers emotional information. Given that the concept of expected utility refers to personal value, the question at hand is: is there any real difference between a rational choice model and a model of intuitive management, except in the additional non-verbal or emotional information that intuitive management purports to be important to collect?

Intuitive management positions itself as an alternative model to that of rational choice by pointing to a series of variables that are made to appear to have little to do with collecting and sifting through evidence and much to do with a complex "instinctive" procedure of processing emotion. The bases of and ways in which people develop expertise have been very extensively studied in many different fields and from many different points of view. Malcolm Gladwell (2005) in the book "Blink" makes a case for the existence of intuitive management and states "decisions made very quickly can be every bit as good as decisions made cautiously and deliberately".[100] Qualified professionals make decisions in an incredibly short amount of time and the author calls this "Thin Slicing". Thin Slicing means that on the basis of accumulated experience in the mass of information that is available in a given interaction, we only focus on a thin slice of this information in order to make a good decision. Let us examine a malpractice suit from an insurer's perspective. Would it be more effective to pore over clinical charts and examine clinical errors for an indication as to whether the physician is likely to be sued for malpractice, or is it more effective to see the physician's relationship style with patients?

The first, the author suggests, while a "rational" approach to the problem does not in fact predict malpractice suits. "Analyses of malpractice lawsuits show that there are highly skilled doctors who get sued a lot and doctors who make lots of mistakes and never get sued".[101] In fact, the majority of people who suffer from poor medical care, do not sue.[102] So the patient being harmed is not a determining factor in malpractice suits, nor is the assiduousness with which doctors treated them a deterrent. Patients file lawsuits because they have been harmed by poor care and because something else has happened. The prevailing literature indicates that patients sue because they feel the physician did not care about them and did not communicate effectively with them.[103, 104] Suing indicates mistrust: how can such data be useful to insurance companies when assessing risk?

By identifying "caring" as a personal value of high standing among patients, using a rational choice model, one could argue that insurance companies are irrationally focusing on non-representative fields of information.

Another example of thin slicing comes from the counseling world. Gottman, who is a marriage therapist, studies couples and is able to predict with 95% accuracy on the basis of a 15-minute dialogue whether a couple will still be married in 15 years' time. The layman has a 53.8% prediction capacity. How does Gottman do this? He thin slices for contempt. While 15 minutes might offer all kinds of data: disgust, anger, defensiveness, whining, sadness, it is the presence of contempt on either person of the couple that determines the failure of the relationship. "Contempt is closely related to disgust, and what disgust and contempt are about is completely rejecting and excluding someone from the community".[105] The interesting thing is that today, Gottman can make this prediction with a high rate of accuracy and needs only 15 minutes to do so. He identified his thin slice by watching thousands of videos of couples in counseling, frame by frame. Thin slicing is an observable phenomenon but its success depends on having spent a great deal of time previously in the process of rational choice of non-verbal information.

Thin slicing is explained by the fact that professionals intuitively select one qualifying element from their experience, which can be interpreted through verbal and non-verbal clues to read the information they are asked to analyse and to make good decisions. Most physicians will describe an amazing diagnosis they made, while they themselves are not sure how they knew what they knew in order to come up with it.

The following case study demonstrates that rational choice and thin slicing are probably one and the same.[106]

Lee Goldman, a cardiologist, generated a very simple algorithm for determining whether an emergency room patient experiencing chest pain should be admitted to the hospital or sent home. This was a very difficult problem for the Emergency Department (ED). There was a big flow of patients to the ED who described intense chest pain. The risk variables were many: age, diet, lifestyle, blood pressure, ECG, smoking, diabetes, etc. The information was so complex that ED physicians kept most patients under-observation convinced that they had made an informed decision. The result was severe overcrowding in the ED.

Goldman instead was convinced that the problem was simpler than it appeared. By running huge amounts of data through a computer model he was able to determine an algorithm that identified the "thin slice" variables that distinguished the emergency from the patient that could be sent home. Goldman's algorithm needed four pieces of information: the ECG results, blood pressure, fluid in the lungs and unstable angina.[107] Physicians as mentioned before, collected many other elements: smoking, weight, lifestyle, previous heart surgery. However all this information in fact reduced the capacity of physicians to distinguish who was and was not having a heart attack.[108]

Faced with a huge ED build up of cardiology cases, the CEO of Cook County Hospital tried to apply Goldman's algorithm. First he had his ED physicians make their own decisions and he charted the results. Then he had them apply Goldman's algorithm in 1996. The algorithm was 70% more effective at recognizing who was not having a heart attack. It was also 6% more effective on determining who was having a serious heart attack than the decision making style his physicians were using.[109]

Intuitive management and thin slicing suggest that models of rational choice are ineffective in making good decisions, because in any situation, a thin slice contains the code of the most effective solution. But Goldman's algorithm is a product of rational choice! Thin slicing has been informed by rational choice.

Thin slicing then is a product of rational choice, it is a shortcut that comes after having used rational choice theories to determine the qualifying position of the thin slice. Intuitive management is not intuitive at all; it is based on the capacity of the decision maker to make a good rational choice.

What intuitive management does introduce, which proves to be particularly important in healthcare is the systematic reading and interpretation of non-verbal information. P. Eckman has conducted extensive scientific studies on facial expressions and their emotional meaning. His work has enabled scientists to begin to document existing facial expressions and affirm that these are homogenous cross-culturally. It is possible to learn to read the "language" of facial expression which gives valuable information as to the emotional states of others.[110]

Irrational patterns of decision making and temporary autism

The down side of the thin slicing theory as it is presented in the intuitive management theory, as an antagonist to the rational choice model, is the role that stereotyping can play in thin slicing. Racist beliefs, and other forms of prejudice may be generated by thin slicing. The author claims that thin slicing is an authoritative form of decision making in the absence of highly emotional states on the part of the decision maker. A decision maker under emotional duress, will significantly endanger the "thin slicing" skill and may under emotional stress make "stereotypical" decisions. The author states, that under emotional duress, the decision maker undergoes an undiagnosed condition, termed "temporary autism". As autism is described as the incapacity to read facial expressions, the emotional condition of the decision maker makes it impossible for him/her to collect the non-verbal information that informs thin slicing. Many cases of racist behaviour on the part of police officers have occurred after high speed chases. In those cities where high speed chases on the part of police officers have been banned, these behaviours have been significantly reduced.

In healthcare, from the emergency room, to any form of health crisis, the emotional condition of the physician and staff will always be subject to "temporary autism". In fact one example of stereotypes of thin slicing in the emergency room, is the mental patient. A patient with a history of mental illness who turns to an emergency room for a heart attack will more often than not, be diagnosed with "a panic attack" and sent to the psychiatric ward. This is an example of how an emergency conjures up stereotypes. This is termed temporary autism for intuitive management and irrational behaviour for rational choice theories, probably an error of representative sampling. It would be interesting to try to work on how to reduce the negative effects of thin slicing, that are the systematic errors which produce irrational behaviour or "temporary autism" among healthcare professionals.

In general, the application of rational choice models to decision making in the field is undoubtedly – and by the admission of the same theorists themselves – of little practical application: "what effect have these findings had on the practice of expert judgment? Almost zilch".[111] The intuitive theory of management is both fascinating and promising as it seems to indirectly subscribe to rational choice; however its language and formulation is more accessible. The big difficulty in the literature is a lack of "common language". In that, while in fact intuitive management subscribes to rational choice modeling, it appears to negate it by emphasizing the speed and accuracy of expert decision makers. In all the examples of "intuitive management" decision makers' abilities were born in a rational choice model. The implications of this debate are clear for healthcare management, rational choice needs to be the basis of healthcare decision making. When this becomes practice, healthcare management will be able to pride themselves on "intuitive thin slicing". Rational choice is the basis for constructing organizational trust. However it will require serious attention at managerial levels to rational choice modeling, to probability and its application and to limiting the hubris of healthcare professionals and managers.

Game theory and rule rationality

Another interesting theory of rationality emerges through game theory studies. In the previous chapter, the prisoner's dilemma and non-cooperative games were discussed. Another way of framing Nash's theory, is to look at social dilemmas and to define "social comparison". Von Neumann and Morgenstern theorized that people should decide based on maximizing utility. The social dilemma presents a twist to this.

If pollution is very bad, it would be better if everyone used public transportation or a bicycle. If I take this seriously and ride my bike to work, but others do not, I will be worse off than if I had taken the car, because while I will be doing what I think is right I will be subject to the consequences of other people's insensitivity to pollution. I compare my outcome, I breathe the fumes of other people's cars, to that of others rather than identifying my expected utility.[112]

Another example of the negative effects of social comparison is:

I have a choice between taking two helpings of dessert and giving my brother one, or having three helpings of dessert and giving my brother four;

from a Von Neumann's theory, presuming I love dessert, I am better off having three desserts and giving my brother four.[113]

In the healthcare organization, the effect of social comparison inside the organization is particularly damaging to the trust paradigm. For example, many patients will request certain diagnostic examinations, because their friend was prescribed it. Organizational culture can be described with the theory of rule rationality.

Rule rationality is an economic idea, it says that people learn good ways to behave and then make these into rules with which to tackle similar situations. People adjust rules when the rules have led them to make mistakes. Milton Friedman's work introduces the concept by affirming that "people behave *as if* they were rational".[114] This means that people give themselves rules of behaviour, they do not act to optimize each single decision. Therefore, a given act is not the result of rational behaviour, but it does reflect the application of a rule or an adjustment to a rule.

Loss, lack or betrayal of trust, in the case of healthcare, is not in the rational best interest of the patient: it is not rationally in the best interest of the patient to discontinue or only partially comply with a therapy, and it is even less in his/her best interest not to report this to the physician. Rule rationality shows that people apply rules of behaviour even if it is not in their best rational interest to do so in that specific act.

Rule rationality can be illustrated with a simple experiment designed by Werner Guth in the 1980s called the "ultimatum game". Two subjects who do not know one another and have no direct contact with one another are given an opportunity to split the equivalent of 200 Euros. Each comes to the setting of the game and leaves through separate entrances and exits. During the game they neither see one another nor hear each other's voice, they send messages through a computer. If they were to meet in the future, neither would know that they had already been involved in a transaction together.

One subject is the donor, the other the receiver. The donor is expected to make an offer to the receiver. If the receiver accepts the donor's first and only offer, both subjects are allowed to keep their respective portion of the 200 Euros. If the receiver refuses the offer, neither will receive the money and the game is over. The donor needs to offer enough for his offer to be accepted, or he will come away with nothing. Expected utility would suggest that it is in the receiver's best interest to accept even 1 Euro, a better outcome than no money at all. However, in the experiment, receivers generally refuse offers under

70 Euros. In some cultures the receiver never accepts an offer from the donor.

The reason a player refuses a win and prefers to walk away with nothing at all, is that the player in the receiver position is not evaluating the specific situation at hand, where there is complete anonymity. The player is looking for the rule of behaviour that would apply to this situation. In a situation where something is to be divided, the rule that people refer to is: don't let yourself be taken advantage of. Word might get around that you are a person who accepts the short end of the stick, then you would have a reputation, and things could only get worse. Getting back to the "ultimatum game", it is a purely anonymous situation, why would a rational person walk away from 50 Euros? The rule rationality principle explains that people give themselves rules of behaviour regardless of whether they are applicable to the particular situation.

In this case the rule is, if someone takes advantage of you, you must fight back and punish them, then they will learn not to do this again. Rule rationality applies equally to both roles in the game. Even the donor knows it exists, and in fact most donors in the experiment offered around 70 Euros (a 65–35% split). Those that offered something significantly lower (an 80–20% split) were generally refused by receivers.[115]

Rule rationality happens in many situations and many different rules apply and override the actual rational judgment that would make sense in the situation at hand. Rule rationality reduces an infinite number of decisions by grouping them together under a rule. Another example is how people on election day respond to polls asking them if they have voted or not. A study in Israel showed that 90% of people polled declared that they had voted. In reality turnout for the election was 68%. Why did people say they had voted? Rule rationality indicates that people believe that when someone you do not know asks you a question, you should be polite. People tend to respond to the person asking the question by trying to tell him/her what he/she wants to hear.

Going back to the case in point, the patient who discontinues therapy or only partially adheres to therapy does indeed damage his/her own health first, just as the receiver of the ultimatum game who refuses 50 Euros, damages his/her own economic situation. The patient also damages the professionalism of his/her physician; the physician has no information as to why the patient is responding to treatment differently than anticipated. If the physician asks "did you take your medication?" the patient, for the same reasons that people respond "yes" to polls asking if they have voted, says "yes". To say you have not taken your medication is not polite nor what the physician wants to hear. This helps to explain why so many patients do not tell their physician how they are really behaving as patients, even though it is not a rational choice in the situation.

Rule rationality is specific to context and to culture, as mentioned before, even in the microcosm of the organization. For example, in a big consulting firm where "staying late" is a cultural norm, people stay in the office until well after dinner. In the morning, at the coffee machine, they exchange war stories about how much they have worked that week. Rule rationality says you are dedicated to the office, your working career and your colleagues if you work 60-hour weeks. Rational judgment would say that it is absurd to stay at work for an extra 20 hours a week, every week, when you are not paid to do so. These same people would not give themselves the rule to stay 12 hours in the park on Sunday. So rule rationality develops in the cultural context of the organization or of a profession.

Apropos of rule rationality in the medical profession, the 2006 Nobel Prize in medicine was awarded to two Australians, Dr. Warren, a pathologist and Dr. Marshall, a gastroenterologist for having identified peptic ulcers as a bacterial infection that could be cured with antibiotics. Physicians were convinced that ulcers resulted from stress and that the stomach was sterile and that nothing could grow in the gastric juices. It was so culturally embedded as a rule, that it was impossible for physicians to see the evidence to the contrary. The bacteria was first identified in 1979, however it took 10 years to make inroads in the rule rationality of the sterile stomach. As Dr. Warren is quoted in the New York Times, "I met skepticism from my colleagues who mostly did not want to know, or believe, what I was describing. Anyone could see the bacteria through a microscope, but the clinicians did not want to see them". Dr. Marshall, during those years saw patients go for surgery and die of internal bleeding. As Dr. Warren puts it "convincing other people was another matter".[116]

Conclusions

The combination of the idea of organizational trust with rational choice and that of rule rationality would indicate that a healthcare organization has to invest in trust and rational choice. Interpersonal trust in the healthcare organization is high; but organizational and public trust are low. The effects of this on patients can be read in patient anxiety, difficulty in assuming self-care behaviours, dependency, non-compliance, alternative therapies and doctor-shopping. Distrust generates stereotyping, temporary autism, and malpractice. From a rule rationality perspective, social comparison generates distrust and all the negative consequences described including stonewalling and hiding errors.

In conclusion, trust is both relationship-based and constructed on models of rational choice. Today, human hubris and the lack of preparation in probability theory on the part of decision makers have led behavioural economists to observe patterns of irrationality rather than of maximization of expected utility in decision making at all levels. In healthcare management, organizational and public trust are particularly damaged by a lack of trust, and this does generate patient distrust in the physician-patient relationship, which in turn, generates large costs both of an economic nature and in terms of quality of care.

Lack of trust in the healthcare organization has high costs in terms of litigation and damages the professional and economic efficacy of the organization. Clinical guidelines for example, while effective if applied in reducing secondary hospital-based infections, do not reduce unnecessary deaths. In the absence of organizational trust and the presence of social comparison – *what will others do to me if I report my own or errors of others?* – betrayal of trust will prevail over trust and rational choice.

New theories on intuitive management, while apparently distant from models of rational choice, reinforce the importance of using rational choice appropriately and add value to these models, especially in the healthcare arena by introducing the importance of non-verbal information. Non-verbal information, like tone and eye contact, may determine more malpractice cases than adhering to clinical guidelines and care paths. Therefore rational choice in healthcare management can be improved by reading non-verbal communication in the organization. Extensive training material exists on recognizing the emotional content of facial expressions and it has been hypothesized that it is possible to learn this language.[117] Rational choice can also limit all irrational patterns of management behaviour from budgeting to sunken costs and compound probability hypotheses. In terms of management development, this will involve extensive exposure to rational choice, expected utility, probability theory, game theory and learning to recognize non-verbal forms of communication in the healthcare setting.

Experienced professionals who build their experience on rational choice models and advanced communication skills will be able through accumulated experience to "thin slice" and make very quick decisions.

There may be implications of these considerations for the selection of healthcare managers. The importance of healthcare-specific experience cannot be overlooked in selecting competent healthcare managers. Good decision makers in the healthcare organization will need to know a great deal of information before they can "thin slice" and this will also depend on the years of experience they have accumulated in studying information, both verbal and non-verbal. Today in Italy, seniority in healthcare management careers has been substituted to make room for merit-based promotion. While seniority in and of itself does not determine experience it is a necessary premise for accumulating it.

Lastly, organizational culture determines rule rationality, and it is important that organizational culture draw from trust and expected utility over mistrust and social comparison.

5
Building Relationships on the Model of Trust

Introduction

This chapter will examine a practical application of the trust model. By building trust it is possible to disclose and learn about the real problems in healthcare management, for patients and physicians. This chapter describes a research project that was designed to build trust with informers and researchers alike, in order to learn about healthcare issues. The research model used the concept of trust not only to design the research question and questionnaires but to support the data collection process itself. This chapter will describe a study in Italy that investigated the communication process between patients and their oncologists over QoL issues. It will describe the importance of the trust model in designing research when patient participation is necessary.

The research question

The purpose of research was to examine the doctor-patient relationship and the trust that patients and physicians had in each other by examining the communication process. The study focused on interpersonal trust, and therefore examined a critical component of the trust relationship: communication. The communication issue that was studied was quality of life (QoL) issues. A patient's trust in his/her physician was measured by asking patients:

- did they experience negative effects of treatment on QoL?
- if so, had they voiced their concerns to the oncologist?
- had there been any response from the professional?

Likewise oncologists were asked to describe their patients' QoL, and whether:

- patients spoke spontaneously about their QoL concerns
- patients' were actively solicited for information about QoL
- patients were given a clinical response.

The research used QoL as a pretext to see how the proposed relationship (the position of the two actors in the communication process) was perceived both by patients and their physicians. The research focused on QoL because, over the last decade, cancer treatments have, in 64.4% of cases, created five-year survival rates of cancer patients, increasing concern over QoL.[118, 119] QoL is also associated with both patient willingness to continue treatment and increased survival.[120, 121] Measuring patient perception of QoL has become common practice; however, little attention has been given to the relationship between oncologists and patients about QoL.[122] As patient perceptions of QoL influence evaluations of care and treatment outcomes, how doctor-patient communication about QoL is managed by oncologists in oncology centres becomes of utmost importance.[123, 124, 125, 126]

QoL issues were conducive to understanding the communication process between patients and physicians because questions concerning patients' QoL could be expressed in simple terms. Therefore, patients from any cultural background could identify whether or not they had perceived negative effects of treatment on their lives, whether they had discussed these with their oncologists and whether speaking up had generated a response. The purpose of the study was not to describe only the QoL of the cancer patient but also to study the communication process around this issue and determine whether this had an effect on the perceived efficacy of treatment. The research question was: how does the proposed relationship between patients and physicians effect the content of their exchange, or the management of QoL?

Two groups of informers, patients and oncologists in oncology centres, provided the data. While the object of the study was the communication process, as a way of describing the interpersonal trust between oncology patients and their physicians, the design of the research process itself was based on the model of trust described in the previous chapter. It focused on building trust between the scientific committee, the sponsor, the university, a patient association, the researchers, the oncology centre and the patients.

Actors in the trust model of designing research

A research project of this kind requires the active participation of organizations and individuals; no single actor or individual can produce the results independent of the group. The university had the knowledge to manage the research design and process, the oncology centres had access to oncologists, the oncologists had accumulated experience with managing cancer patients, the nurses, oncologists, patients and psychologists had competence in the QoL of the oncology patients, the patient association had access to researchers with the necessary sensitivity to conduct the research. The study also had to be financed to be realized. In this case, the research was sponsored by a pharmaceutical company.

The model of trust was applied in building the professional network among these actors. The trust model states that it is necessary to activate trust when risk is involved. All of the actors had to assume risks in order to realize the project. As described in the previous chapter, trust is a necessary component of a relationship where there is perceived risk. In the absence of risk, there is no need for trust.

Risk for patients

In this case, the research question evoked risk for patients and necessitated patient trust. Patients in the study were currently undergoing chemotherapy and were in the care of the oncology centre. They were being asked whether they communicated their symptoms to their physicians. The risk for patients was that if they declared their true responses, this would somehow be negatively reflected in the quality of care accorded to them in the future. It was necessary that patients trust the process and researchers, so that the quality of results would not be affected by fear of negative consequences in the care process. From their perspective, the care process lasted for many years after chemotherapy was over: oncology patients with successful results undergo five years of follow-up examinations. If these present no recurrent cancer episodes, the patient is considered cured of the cancer episode. The risk was that patients would respond, but using rule rationality, asking themselves what their caretakers wanted to hear. They would feel uncomfortable about revealing communication problems around QoL and that would deteriorate the quality of the data.

Risk for the sponsor

The sponsor of the research was a pharmaceutical company that produced a drug for treating cancer-related anemia and therefore, the study, in order to be financed, required an investigation of cancer-related fatigue. The pharmaceutical company was interested in raising patient awareness in cancer-related fatigue. The term fatigue was completely unknown in the patient population in Italy and in the international literature, the symptom was important. The hypothesis of the pharmaceutical company was that patients kept fatigue symptoms to themselves, assuming that they were not treatable or were issues that could not be discussed, unlike other QoL issues such as nausea and pain. The pharmaceutical company was interested in a study that would legitimize this symptom by giving it a name and would thereby encourage patients to speak up. This, in turn, would encourage physicians to discuss and eventually treat it.

As the sponsor had a direct interest in the results of the research, it was important that the research remain independent of the sponsor's influence. The sponsor risked financing a project that would not meet its goals of raising consciousness around cancer-related fatigue as an important and under-recognized area of QoL for the cancer patient undergoing chemotherapy.

Risk for the patient association and researchers

The researchers were going to be the only actors speaking to the patients directly. They needed to be able to respond to any patient concern and trust that what they affirmed was true. The researchers had to trust that the research process was not being manipulated and that data would not be subject to unexpected uses.

Risk for the university

For the university, the risk was that the research question would generate a homogeneous response that everything was perfect in patient-physician communication. The other risk was that oncology centres would not participate in the study, impeding the study's realization. Also, oncology centres may not be interested in taking the time to recruit patients.

There was also a credibility risk. The former editor of the New England Journal of Medicine, Marcia Angell, published a best selling "whistle blowing" book on the influence of pharmaceutical companies on medical research. The examples presented indicate that the pharmaceutical industry exercises a level of influence over scientific methods that go from directing research to threatening physicians by taking away grant money if they publish negative results.[127]

In this case the research institute was responsible for framing and responding to the sponsor's needs, and also for guaranteeing that the sponsor's level of influence over research would not compromise the results obtained.

The alternative to working with the pharmaceutical sponsor was to do nothing. The problem was interesting and the process was complicated. In Italy, there are no alternative public resources for this type of research. The trust model was a critical tool for working ethically within these constraints.

How trust informed the research data collection design

Trust is forward looking, and most of the time, people use some form of rational choice when choosing someone to trust. It is not enough to build trust on "what you say you will do". Elements of rational choice have to qualify the trust paradigm: does the trustee possess the competence, the experience, and other measurable variables to inform the trust model. The next section will discuss the roles of all the actors in the research design and implementation process.

Numerous encounters with the pharmaceutical company enabled the university to design a study that would address a wider theme than that initially requested. Initially, the sponsor requested a study on "cancer-related fatigue". Asking patients only about fatigue, and then declaring that it was the most important unaddressed area of QoL, when research was sponsored by a pharmaceutical company whose product addressed cancer-related anemia, was not going to be a credible process. The university proposed a study on communication around "QoL". The sponsor agreed to this and assumed a risk: that cancer-related fatigue would prove unimportant to patients as compared with nausea, pain and depression.

A multi-professional scientific committee was created to select and construct research materials. Members included a chief oncologist, a head nurse of oncology, a recovered cancer patient, a cancer patient, two psychologists who work with an association for breast cancer patients and two researchers from the research institute. The chief oncologist, head nurse and patients all belonged to different oncology centres. Furthermore the patient association saw patients from all the different hospitals in the Milan area.

As a first step, existing scientifically validated questionnaires on cancer-related fatigue and on QoL were examined by the scientific committee. As the scientific committee examined the different scientifically validated scales for measuring fatigue: the Rhoten Fatigue Scale, the Piper Fatigue Self-report scale, the Pearson-Byars Fatigue Checklist, the Multi-dimensional Fatigue Inventory, the Fatigue Symptom Inventory, the Brief Fatigue Inventory and the Schwartz Cancer Fatigue Scale, each one presented one or all of the following problems: the scale had been validated and had only been used in English-speaking countries, the formulation of the questions was complicated to understand, and there were no adjustments for cultural specificity. Some of these tests had a 30% patient refusal to complete them.[128]

The questionnaires had another two problems. First, they focused on QoL assessment and did not examine the communication process between the patient and the oncologist, and second, the questionnaires' language implied that a professional would have to propose the questionnaire directly to the patient so that the patient could understand the question. For example, the literature suggests "three simple questions" for determining cancer-related fatigue; these were:

"Are you experiencing any fatigue? If yes how severe has it been using a 1–10 scale? How is the fatigue inferring with your ability to function?"[129] In Italy the word "fatigue" is completely unknown to the general population. Patients would not have understood the question. Other scales that analysed QoL had not developed, according to the scientific literature, an adequate investigation of cancer-related fatigue.

The scientific committee had to investigate QoL, including cancer-related fatigue, and stimulate the patient to disclose whether he/she communicated these symptoms and whether he/she received a response. In this case it was not reasonable to imagine that the issue of communication with the patient could be investigated by the same people whom patients were depending on for their care. The patient had to be able to complete the questionnaire without professional assistance. Patients were not well, therefore, the questionnaire had to be "quick, easy and relevant". Furthermore, how the items were expressed needed to encourage the patient to communicate. The fact that in some cases existing validated questionnaires had caused a 30% patient refusal to complete them was not acceptable as a starting point.

The scientific committee, on the basis of this evaluation of existing research questionnaires, decided to construct a questionnaire that would specifically address the research question: investigate patient perception of QoL, oncologists' perception of the same issue, and the communication process. Therefore, the committee agreed that the design of the study had to begin with trusting the patient.

From a clinical point of view it was possible to collect physical evidence of QoL issues, for example, if a patient declares that he/she feels tired, the clinicians might watch him/her walk up three flights of stairs. However, the multi-disciplinary committee agreed that the effect of this complaint of tiredness on the patient's expectations and lifestyle should not be measured clinically, except by letting the patient describe his/her perception. The committee also agreed that any questionnaire that required any kind of clinical follow-up: data from the patient's chart, a blood or stress test, demonstrated a lack of trust in patient declarations and would have deteriorated the patient relationship with the oncology centre. Put in simple terms, if the patient declared nausea, no physician required evidence of vomiting to prescribe anti-nausea medication. There was a reason for this practice: patients would have felt that their physician did not trust their declarations. This scientific committee therefore assumed that the patient was the true informer as to his/her QoL, as QoL was deemed to be subjectively and not objectively measurable.

Two questionnaires were designed in order to measure the communication process around QoL as perceived in patients treated with chemotherapy and the perception of oncology centres of patient communication.

The areas of QoL that were identified and explored to study the communication process between patients and oncologists were: cancer-related fatigue, nausea, pain, and depression.

The specific Italian context was taken into consideration in preparing the questionnaire itself, as communication processes are culturally based.[130, 131, 132] The scientific committee worked to design a questionnaire by listening to the patient experience. While only two patients participated in the scientific committee, they subjectively expressed their experience. The oncologist, nurse and psychologists used these subjective descriptions to review and share their professional experience which had involved the treatment of many patients. This created a process in which there was an active discussion of those subjective experiences that seemed extendable to a larger patient base and those which seemed personal and unique. The team looked for overlap between the subjective description of the two patient members and the professional common experience.

Lastly, the screening form admitted patients with lung, breast, ovarian and colon cancer, in phase 2, currently undergoing chemotherapy. In choosing which oncology patients to include in the study, the scientific committee was subject to meeting interests of various stakeholders. That is to say, if it did not examine cancer-related fatigue, the research would not be financed, furthermore, in order to make the process work, the committee needed a network. The committee had the support of a patient association specialized in breast cancer, not only for the design of the research materials but also for collecting data. The design of research in this case, had to take into account the interests of its support network. Therefore, in exchange for this support, two out of the four cancers were typically female cancers: breast and ovarian.

Research process design: privacy and "human subjects"

The research was designed to reach a significant sample of oncology centres and patients and to respect the Italian privacy laws. Italian privacy laws determine that the patient must give written consent to participate in a study of this kind. Specifically, the research institute wrote to all oncology centres in Italy asking for their participation, each oncology centre which accepted was asked to collect ten consecutive patients. This involved collecting signed "release of private information" forms from patients with the characteristics required by the study. These forms indicated the patient's name and phone number and authorized the university to contact them to explain the study. It was not an agreement to participate. This took a large part of the burden of recruitment of human subjects away from the oncology centres and put it directly into the hands of the research institute. The oncology centre was simply to provide contact information.

When the centre had collected the ten consecutive patient "release of private information" forms, and had completed the questionnaire for the oncologists, these were mailed to the university. In some cases, the centres required that the study be approved by the committee on ethics. In no case did the committee on ethics refuse participation.

At this point, the researchers phoned patients explaining the purpose of the study and asked the patient to participate. If the patient agreed to participate in the study, the research institute sent the questionnaire to their homes and asked them to complete it and send it back to with a signed consent form that allowed the university to use the data to construct the database. The patient was contacted again to make sure that he/she had received the material and to clear up any difficulties they may have had with the questionnaire. When the completed form arrived, the patient was thanked by the research team.

The process involved four pieces of mail for each patient: sending the information to the oncology centre, receiving it from the centre, sending it to the patient and receiving it from the patient. The Italian postal service sometimes delivered next day, and other times mail took two months. This accounted for some unanticipated delays. 40 patients of the 1,014 patients contacted, had died when the questionnaire arrived at their homes which explains how the phase 2 cancer diagnosis as an inclusion criterion did not always reflect the actual condition of the patient. The clinical condition of the patient was not homogeneous in the sample due to the privacy laws and the postal service. The process began at the beginning of February 2002 and was concluded in October 2002.

Collecting the data: issues of trust

The research institute designed a process that guaranteed that both oncology centre and patient responses would go directly to and from the university. This helped to guarantee patients the anonymity of their responses. It was important to propose a trusting relationship with the patient. This guarantee, however, was not of great significance to the patient; they were not familiar with research protocols or university ethics and policies. From the patient's perspective, patients needed and would continue to need the care of the oncologists in the oncology centre. There needed to be a guarantee to the patient that the university would not share individual results with the oncology centre. The patient had to trust the researcher with very sensitive information.

Besides making sure that individual patient responses were kept separate from their oncology centres, the sensitive nature of the information requested of the patients required special attention to the contact between the researchers and the patients. The design of the flow of information in and of itself was not enough.

Seven field researchers who were themselves ex-cancer patients were selected from the association for patients with breast cancer to create a field team. These researchers had all been healthy for the last five years, however, they were personally familiar with the physical, psychological and family issues associated with having cancer. To protect the field team from burn-out and to give them the professional skills to undertake the research, the field team underwent 12 hours of specific training in communication to enable them to professionally contact chief oncologists and patients.

The research goals were shared with the team, and the questionnaires were discussed so that the team was prepared to handle questions. Team building among field researchers was constant: meetings took place once every ten days to share progress, problems and solutions as they arose. The first and foremost issue of trust that arose with the research team was the role of the pharmaceutical company as the sponsor in the research process. As ex-patients they were extremely sensitive and wary of the role of the pharmaceutical company in the process, and were concerned about presenting themselves to patients as trustworthy when they themselves did not trust the sponsor. This issue was addressed in numerous meetings both with and without the presence of the sponsor. These actions built trust among field researchers, the university and the sponsor. The sponsor guaranteed that its objective was to raise consciousness around an important unaddressed symptom. Furthermore, the scientific literature clearly stated that the product did not in fact address cancer-related fatigue as a whole, but was beneficial in the event that cancer-related fatigue was accompanied by anemia, and positively effected only about half of those cases. Trust was built on mutual interests between the researchers and the sponsor.

Researchers were painfully aware of the effects of chemotherapy on QoL, they had been through it themselves. They also knew that talking about these perceptions to your physician is extremely difficult. The pharmaceutical company wished to raise consciousness about how patients perceive fatigue. This was an objective that the researchers believed in.

Building the trust relationship with the sponsor was based in part on the scientific literature, but was requested and maintained as an interpersonal trust relationship between the corporate representative and the research team.

Each member of the research team contacted about 140 patients. Each researcher during the course of the study required "time off" as the emotional burden of the project was difficult to handle for many consecutive months. Each field researcher requested and received time off as needed.

Managing trust turned out to be a critical issue in the data collection process. The field team worked with patients and their families: 72% of the patients contacted had phone calls screened by family members who would not let an unknown person and project be presented to the patients themselves. They were the gatekeepers; they protected the patient. The field team kept research notes about their phone calls, and learned a great deal beyond their own personal experience, about how families protect their members. One requirement for achieving high patient involvement was to build trust with the patient's family first, and only later with the patient. Often family members answered the phone call and requested information about the study themselves. In larger families, the researcher was asked to call back until every involved family member had approved the research, and only then was the researcher allowed to speak directly with the patient.

Other family members requested that the material be sent to them so they could review it first or be sure that the patient be presented with the questionnaire when he/she felt well enough to fill it out. One patient said of her family "I know this is the third time you are sending me the questionnaire, they keep throwing it away!" Hundreds of patients used the phone call to tell their stories, saying that they were relieved to talk to an outsider as they did not want to further upset family members. Some asked to be called back because "it will mean I am still alive".

Elderly patients were afraid that they would not be able to follow the questionnaire. They were reassured and were called for any extra assistance they felt they needed. The team worked with the empathy that was natural from their own experience, their understanding of the objectives of the research, and the training in communication that they received, to gain the trust of the family and work directly with patients.

Both patients and oncology centres filled out the questionnaire unassisted and mailed it back to the university. The results in terms of response rate were exceptional: the study contacted 180 oncology centres in all regions of Italy, and 110 joined the study (61% response). These centres provided 1,014 names of patients with valid phone numbers. Of these, 40 patients had died before they could be contacted. A total of 790 patients responded to the questionnaire (81% response).

Implications of the high response rate

Studies of the importance of response rate in influencing the statistical significance of data have found that response rates increase as the research organization invests in developing the contact with the target population. Callbacks, shorter questionnaires and salience of the research to the target population are some of the tools described for positively increasing response rates to mail questionnaires. However, the research on response rates argues that these have an impact on the time it takes to complete the study and on the cost of the study itself. While it is agreed that "Higher cooperation, legitimately obtained, should improve the quality of the sample"[133] it has also been found that a higher response rate may have no statistically significant impact on the data. That is, the data confirms the same message even at lower response rates. In fact the Centre for Disease Control and Prevention (CDC) reported on an overall trend in CDC average response rates from 71.4% in 1993 to 48.9% in 2000, a 35.5% drop. In a separate study on smoking habits in Nevada there was a 45% drop in response rate which produced "a predicted difference in smoking prevalence rates of 1.5 percentage points".[134] So while the response rate attests to the quality of the sample, it generally does not significantly influence the quality of the data.

The response rate in this case indicates the high quality of the sample and it was obtained through a practical application of the model of trust used to design the field study. The high response rate can be explained in one of two ways. The first is the high interest in the subject. This is known as the "salience" of the research questions: salience is described as the importance or timeliness of a specific topic with the target population.[135] Obviously, QoL is a salient issue among patients diagnosed with cancer and undergoing chemotherapy. However, all research studies presume to study issues of interest to the target population. In studies of this kind the average response rate is around 30%. In other validated questionnaires on QoL the refusal rate of the target population to complete the questionnaire was 30% despite the fact that the issue was salient.

The trust model used the patient experience to construct the salience of the questionnaire. This enabled the questionnaire to communicate the issues "as the patient felt them and would have expressed them" and to identify the areas that patients would feel were most important. The trust model was extremely valuable in creating salience as it went beyond simply researching a "topic of interest" to ensure patient identification with the issues.

The research team trusted the university and the sponsor. This occurred both through sharing information: the questionnaire itself and the goals of the sponsor as to the uses to which results would be directed. The information collected was not particularly time sensitive and the time it took to reach 790 patients was not, as can be the case in research studying "current events", a variable that needed to be managed in a short period of time.

In general, this study proposed to describe organizational efficacy and its effect on patient health. The response rate points to the importance of the trust model in constructing data collection that involves patient participation.

The questionnaire

The questionnaire addressed the same items to both patients and oncology centres. It was formulated so that patients of different educational and social backgrounds could easily respond. The research team based the differentiation between fatigue and depression on the International Classification of Disease (ICD10) proposed by the World Health Organization. In the questionnaire, fatigue was distinguished from depression, though the two areas are very related, by placing an emphasis on physical exhaustion as distinguished from items which only addressed the patient's state of mind.[136, 137, 138, 139]

Items of the questionnaire contained the following statements, to which the patient was to respond: always, sometimes or never. Patients were also asked whether they communicated these symptoms (always, sometimes, never) to their oncologists and how often (always, sometimes, never) and what kind of response they received from them (*"it's a normal part of the illness and its treatment"*, or treatment for the symptom):

Pain
- I feel such pangs of pain that I have no desire to do anything
- Pain is constant and is a part of my day

Fatigue
- I feel too physically exhausted to get out of bed in the morning
- I don't have the physical strength to participate in those activities that used to interest me (eg: tennis, work, cinema)
- I am so physically exhausted that it is difficult for me to begin and finish the little things in life (walk up a flight of stairs, shop at the supermarket)

Depression
- I feel no desire to begin the day
- It is difficult to begin and end even the little things in life because I do not feel like doing anything (write a letter, phone a friend, read the newspaper)

Nausea

- I have a sense of nausea even when I am not near food
- I taste different tastes in food that I know
- I vomit

Part 2 of the questionnaire asked patients whether they spoke to others about these issues, and Part 3 enquired as to the specific types of responses they received from oncologists.

The items in the questionnaire were identical for oncology centres and for patients. Oncology centres had to describe whether their patients were experiencing these QoL issues, how often and what was being done to respond to these.

Results

790 patients were recruited: 35.1% of patients were male, 64.9% were female. 27.3% of patients declared lung cancer, 8.0% ovarian, 34.6% breast, 23.7% colon. 6.4% of respondents did not know or remember their diagnosis. Average age of the patient sample was 58.7 years (±10.8). Education levels were as follows: elementary school certificate 9.4%, junior high school diploma 52.7%, high school diploma 27.5%, college degree 9.4%, post graduate 1.1%. 96% of patients live with their families, 1.2% live alone, and 2.8% live with a person who assists.

In *Graph 5.1*, 89.5% of patients declared that they suffered from fatigue, 86.2% from nausea, 73.6% from pain, and 73.4% from depression. Patients expressed cancer-related fatigue as the principal invalidating condition on their QoL. 45.6% of patients suffered constantly (always) from fatigue, 28.7% from nausea, 17.7% from pain, and 24.8% from depression. This research highlights a relationship between fatigue and depression and an area of convergence (chi-squared of Pearson $p < 0.0005$, coefficient of contingency=0.51). 70.7% of patients report that they feel both fatigue and depression, 2.7% only depression, 18.8% only fatigue, 7.8% neither depression nor fatigue.

40.3% of patients "always" spoke about fatigue to their oncologist, 44.8% about nausea, 38.7% about pain, and 20.4% about depression. Some patients never voice their concerns: 16.1% fatigue, 13.3% nausea, 5.6% pain and 24.4% depression. In the cases of nausea and pain patients report symptoms with insistence even if they occur only sometimes. In the cases of fatigue and depression, patients under-report symptoms that are always present.

In *Graph 5.2*, patients speak more with the oncologist and their families than they do with the other typical healthcare figures present

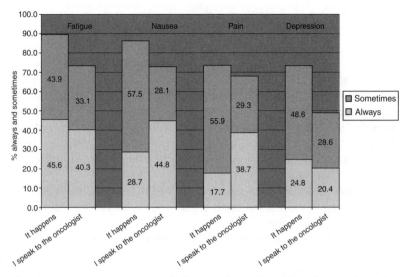

Graph 5.1 Patient perception: "It happens" and "I speak to the oncologist" – fatigue, nausea, pain and depression

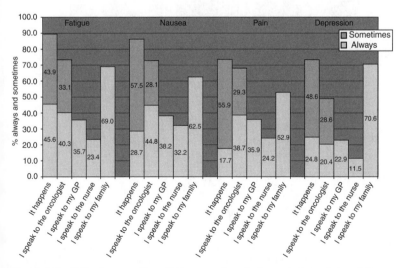

Graph 5.2 Patient perception: "It happens" and whom do I speak to – fatigue, nausea, pain and depression

in their care process: 69% of patients speak to their families about fatigue, 62.5% about nausea, 52.9% about pain, and 70.6% about depression. 35.7% of patients voice their concerns with the GP about fatigue, 38.2% about nausea, 35.9% about pain, 22.9% about depression. 23.4% speak with the nurses in oncology wards about fatigue, 32.2% about nausea, 24.2% about pain, and 11.5% about depression.

Considering the total of always and sometimes represented in *Graph 5.3*, 99% of oncologists declare that they ask patients about fatigue, 100% about nausea and pain and 91% about depression. 100% of oncologists declare that patients report fatigue, nausea and pain, and 98.1% depression.

In *Graph 5.4*, 29.5% of patients declare that they always receive treatment for symptoms of fatigue with 65.2% for nausea, 53.4% for pain, 14.8% for depression.

In the cases of nausea and pain, oncology centres prescribe treatment in the absence of patient symptoms and of patient communication. The chi-squared test shows a significant association between the presence of symptoms and the treatment received (χ^2 = 33.24; p < 0.0005 and χ^2 = 108.60; p < 0.0005 respectively): 6.8% of patients

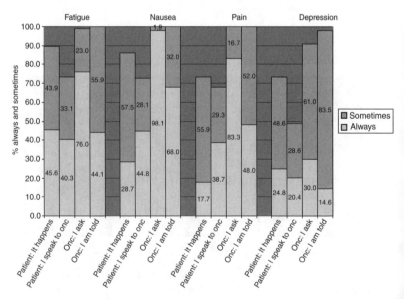

Graph 5.3 Patient-oncologist perceptions: Comparison of patient "It happens" "I speak to the oncologist" and the oncologist "I ask" or "I am told" – fatigue, nausea, pain and depression

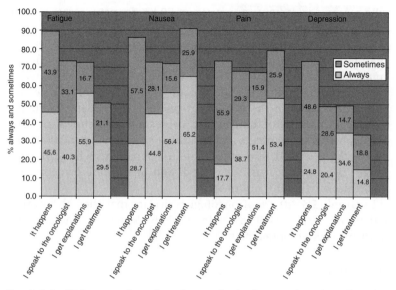

Graph 5.4 "It happens, I speak to the oncologist, I get explanations, I receive treatment" – fatigue, nausea, pain and depression

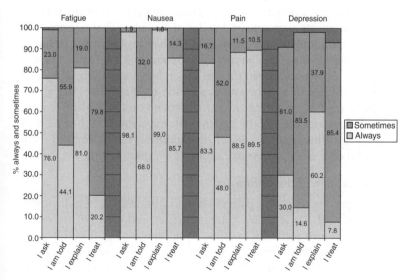

Graph 5.5 Oncologist perceptions: I ask, I am told, I explain, I treat – fatigue, nausea, pain and depression

who received treatment for nausea and 9.8% for pain, received treatment in the absence of symptoms.

In the cases of fatigue and depression, patients declare a gap between symptoms and treatment of 38.9% and 39.8% respectively. There is smaller gap between patients who declare that they communicate symptoms of fatigue and depression and their perception of receiving treatment; 22.8% in the case of fatigue and 15.4% depression. The statistical analysis for fatigue and depression also shows an association between symptoms and treatment (χ^2 = 25.91; p < 0.0005 and χ^2 = 10.23; p = 0.001 respectively): 46.6% of patients who experience fatigue declare that it is not treated, and in the case of depression 63.0% declare that it is not treated.

In *Graph 5.5*, 20.2% of oncologists declare that they always treat fatigue, 85.7% nausea, 89.5% pain and 7.8% depression. There is a gap in the perception of treatment.

Discussion

The data presented here show that the principal actors in the process – oncologists and patients – express great interest in the issue of QoL. Patient response figures indicate patient interest in QoL issues, and the data concerning oncologist perception show great attention to the QoL of patients. Both patient and oncologist data show that the interpersonal relationship is secondary to clinical evidence. That is, oncologists look for symptoms and treat symptoms that appear in the literature, the interpersonal patient-physician relationship is treated as a product of scientific evidence – even though QoL is by nature a subjective experience.[140, 141, 142, 143] Fatigue and depression represent the critical areas in the treatment of QoL because they depend on the subjective difference (before and after) of the patient's life experience on the one hand, and on the other, there are fewer clinical certainties in terms of a standard and effective response to complaints in these realms.

The perception of the oncologist

Oncologists perceive that patients fully communicate their discomfort regarding QoL issues: 100% fatigue, nausea and pain, 98.1% depression. Oncologist response to questionnaires indicates that the QoL of patients is important. In all four areas, oncologists perceive that they treat almost all symptoms: 100% fatigue, nausea and pain, 93.2% depression. Oncologist perceptions show that as caregivers they feel concern and interest for patient QoL.

The perception of patients

Two forms of patient resignation to an unsatisfactory QoL are illustrated in this study. The first concerns those patients who do not voice their discomforts though they feel repercussions on their lifestyle: 16.1% fatigue, 13.3% nausea, 5.6% pain and 24.4% depression. Total resignation of patients is more present around the areas of fatigue and depression than it is around the areas of nausea and pain. The patient prefers to speak to the oncologist and to the family about QoL rather than to the other "technical" figures: nurses and general practitioners. Patients are reluctant to insist with the oncologist and communicate discomfort: the patient experience is never fully communicated. In the cases of nausea and pain, patients communicate around symptoms that they feel always and some that they feel only sometimes, while in the cases of fatigue and depression patients do not always communicate symptoms even when they feel them "always". 89.5% of patients experience fatigue and 73.4% depression, these are largely under-communicated and under-treated.

In the case of nausea and pain, patients are always treated even if they have no symptoms. All patients are aware of receiving treatment, 28.7% declare that they always feel nausea and 17.7% declare that they always feel pain. 57.5% and 55.9% declare that they feel nausea and pain "sometimes".

The gap in perception: patient and oncologist

The gap between oncologist's perception of patient communication and patient's perception of patient communication is 26.6% for fatigue, 27.1% nausea, 32% pain, 48.9% depression. The data indicate that oncologists may not be listening to the subjective experience of their patients, but may be listening instead to the scientific research around QoL in studies of patients. 86.2% of patients experience nausea and 91.1% declare that they receive treatment, 73.6% experience pain and 79.3% receive treatment. These figures indicate that oncologists are prescribing treatment for nausea and pain even when the patient has no symptoms of these. According to patient data, oncologists over-prescribe corrective medication for pain and for nausea. This would indicate that oncologists do not tend to base their prescriptions in these areas on patient communication of their symptoms, but rather on scientific knowledge of the presence of these symptoms in cancer patients undergoing chemotherapy. Furthermore, oncologists always prescribe medication for nausea and pain even if patient symptoms are not constant: 28.7% of patients always feel nausea, 65.2% always receive treatment, 17.7% of patients always feel pain and 53.4% always receive treatment.

The patient on the other hand recognized that treatment for nausea and pain had been received. If a protocol exists that expects that all patients undergoing chemotherapy will experience nausea and pain, then all patients will be given a prescription ex-ante in the event that they experience these. This would explain how patients receive therapy for nausea and pain even in the absence of symptoms. The data also shows how clinical protocols can overcome the problem of communication. Even those patients who did not communicate a symptom were provided with treatment.

However, the study asked the patient to express his/her perception of experience. Their subjective nausea and pain is present both always and sometimes in 86.2% (nausea) and 73.6% (pain). One conclusion might be that anti-nausea and pain medication are substantially inadequate in treating symptoms, however the scientific literature on these therapies indicates otherwise. This result may indicate that an anticipated response to a probable symptom does not have a "perceived efficacy" even though the treatment has a proven clinical efficacy. In the absence of a subjective exchange and adjustment of therapy, only 13.8% (nausea) and 26.4% (pain) declared that they perceive the efficacy of treatment.

These figures indicate that oncologist's perception of patient QoL is based on "clinical knowledge" rather than on the communication of the subjective experience of the single patient. The oncologist is very responsive where clinical solutions exist but directs the proposed relationship with patients through scientific evidence.

Patients are aware of a prescriptive practice in these areas that is not connected to the communication of symptoms and in some cases a prescriptive practice that exists in the absence of symptoms. Listening to specific patient communication emerges as a weak area in all four areas of QoL. This model of the doctor-patient relationship represents an attempt to relieve all patient symptoms, which is desirable; however, it indicates a lack of appropriateness in some cases, a lack of effectiveness in most cases, and a solution in only 13.8% (nausea) and 26.4% (pain) of patient experience.

In the case of depression and fatigue, patients are aware that their symptoms go unattended. Patients describe a gap between symptoms and treatment of 38.9% for fatigue and 39.8% for depression. 45.6% of patients always experience fatigue and only 29.5% always receive treatment. 24.8% always experience depression and only 14.8% always receive treatment. Patients perceive major differences in the oncologist's approach to nausea and pain from fatigue and depression. Fatigue and depression appear to be harder to diagnose and correct from a scientific perspective. Therefore, oncologists are objectively unable to relieve unpleasant symptoms in QoL in these areas.

Conclusion

The data from the study indicates that oncologists do feel that QoL issues in all areas are important and concern them directly. However, the patient-oncologist relationship around QoL issues appears to be based on scientific protocols rather than on patient perception,[144, 145, 146, 147] though it is largely agreed that QoL is a subjective issue.

This research implies that fatigue and depression are under-communicated and generally not responded to when the cancer patient does express them. Furthermore, the data indicates that for a more appropriate management of the QoL of cancer patients undergoing chemotherapy in all areas, it is necessary to base care on the subjective experience of the patient. This, however, produces consequences for hospital organization. The organizational model has not been fully explored in its potential for creating a trusting container for the patient.

The data indicates that there appears to be little collaboration between different professional categories (oncologists, GPs and nurses) around QoL of cancer patients undergoing chemotherapy. Since the organization does not orient and manage patient communication around QoL issues, the patient decides whom to turn to: the oncologist. QoL could be explored as an organizational goal for all professional figures: with attention to patient subjectivity becoming not only a communication skill but an organizational paradigm. Furthermore, the patient's family is the principal container of patient experience about QoL. The family is an organization that listens but does not have the skills to act. However, patients turn to their families anyway. This may indicate that part of the response to QoL issues is creating a context in which the patient can voice them.

Clinical solutions, in this case nausea and pain medication as ex-ante measures to guarantee patient QoL, are not sufficient to guarantee perceived quality of care. Alone, they do not eliminate the perceived risk of symptoms on the part of patients. The Italian Oncology Division organization has chosen to work with clinical protocols to eliminate risk and therefore foster cooperation. The perceived risk of negative symptoms is not eliminated with clinical solutions alone. The perceived efficacy of the clinical solution is missing the interpersonal trust relationship that accounts for the subjective perception of treatment efficacy.

Critical issues for forward-looking trust-based indicators

The research method which designed a process based on trust produced an extremely high response rate. Where patients are asked to participate in clinical research it is important that the research process itself be constructed on the basis of trust. It produces a high response rate and a quality sample.

This study on perceived QoL identifies the need to construct an integrated model between clinical protocol and oncology centre-patient relationship. While prescribing anti-nausea and pain medication ex-ante is an effective way to overcome patient reluctance to report symptoms, follow-up checks with the patient to collect patient perception of the perceived efficacy of treatment and adjustment of treatment to meet the subjective experience are necessary to guarantee full clinical efficacy and build trust between the patient and the oncology centre.

Lastly, the family is a collector of patient information. There are more than 25 million family caregivers in the United States and they are consistently perceived by healthcare organizations as "difficult". In a study published in Annals of Internal Medicine physicians indicated families as the number one source of "difficulty" in managing patients. "A persistent tendency is evident, in both the literature and the practice of healthcare delivery, to equate families with trouble".[148] Families are typically advocates for the patient, and therefore are often perceived as breaking organizational rules and protocols by physicians. The research on QoL in Italian patients shows that families are often the preferred depositories of patient information, more than the oncologist and much more than nurses and GPs. The research process captured their role as gatekeepers in reaching the patient him/herself. Structuring the QoL process to include patients and their caregivers could foster trust and perceived efficacy of treatment.

These observations identify organizational strategies that can build trust and encourage new contexts in which to build paradigms of rule rationality. Thinking about organization as a tool with which to bolster trust and effect rational choice systematically may both increase perceived clinical efficacy and reduce costs. While the research addressed oncology specifically, the implications of the trust-building organizational model may be applied to all clinical divisions. As trust is a forward-looking indicator it proves a more cost effective policy in everything from risk management to malpractice suits and managerial control systems.

6
Managerial Competence: Peer to Peer Relationship Management Skills

Introduction

The previous chapters have identified aspects of the healthcare organization that render the management function in this context an area of specialization with specific critical issues. The implication of the analysis is that management experience in other sectors and management tools need to be modelled and adapted to meet the healthcare challenge. In this chapter, the specific characteristics of the healthcare organization will be translated from characteristics that qualify the organization as special to the characteristics that make the management role special. The competence necessary for the healthcare manager will be explored. Two managerial roles will be identified: the healthcare professional and the manager.

The specificity of healthcare management role: the changing context

This section will explore the context in which the manager is acting. Communication theory affirms "a phenomenon remains unexplainable as long as the range of observations is not wide enough to include the context in which the phenomenon occurs".[149] To illustrate this point, let us take the homeless problem in the United States. From the City Hall perspective, this is a problem of providing temporary food and shelter for the homeless.

Enormous sums of money are spent on temporary shelters and on food kitchens. A cot alone, a few inches away from another cot, costs New York City US $24,000 a year.[150] However, if the homeless problem is looked at only from the City's point of view

> the consumption of resources is grossly under-estimated. In Boston, for example, the medical expenses of 119 homeless people were tracked over a five-year period. In this period 33 of these people died and seven were sent to a nursing home. Together they accounted for 18,834 emergency room visits at a minimum cost of a US $1,000 a visit.[151] In five years the cost of managing those 119 people (this counts the cost of temporary shelter and medical care) amounted to US $419,000 per person, and nothing that the City has done to invest in food and temporary shelter has changed the nature of the phenomenon.

City Hall, without tracking medical expenses, has no view of the real costs of homelessness. The phenomenon is escaping the range of observation, and homelessness remains unexplainable, unsolvable and expensive. This example illustrates the importance of making explicit the context in interpreting a phenomenon, in this case, the field of managerial action in healthcare.

The classical theory of the managerial field focuses on the manager in the hierarchy. Managers work in a pyramid. The manager generally reports to a boss, and at the highest levels to a board, and organizes subordinates and resources. In an early description of the managerial function the following elements were identified:[152]

- hierarchical structure of control authority and communication
- specialized differentiation
- identification of individual tasks
- reconciliation of individual tasks into clusters for each level of the hierarchy
- definition of rights and obligations
- vertical interaction between subordinates and management
- governing by superiors
- obedience to superiors as a condition of membership
- value of internal knowledge

As can be seen the focus of the managerial function is predominantly hierarchical with attention to the up and down flow of information between managers and their subordinates in the pyramid. In fact even in the "how-to" literature on management, more popular among practitioners than theoretical management papers, the emphasis is on managing subordinates and in some cases some advice is given on managing your boss. The concept in how-to books is that the manager is called to achieve results through others using authority. These books give the reader advice as to how to be successful in the hierarchy.

All organizations are hierarchies, but the organization today is exclusively concentrated on its up down side. It pays no attention to its horizontal side. Because of this concentration on the up and down, the biggest problems organizations face can be seen in the tendency of information, problems and decisions to travel up the vertical path of the hierarchy and mushroom at the top. While in theory the role of the manager is to plan, organize, decide and evaluate, this mushroom effect of little and big things rolling upwards takes its toll on the manager. On the how-to list, this mushroom effect has led to best selling titles like "Don't do, delegate", "The One Minute Manager", etc. Mintzberg in a study of what CEOs really do discovered that "half the activities engaged in by the five chief executives of my study lasted less than nine minutes and only ten percent exceeded an hour".[153]

The popular "reengineering" revolution of organization discussed in the first chapter, tried to fix this by focusing on simplification. The novelty of reengineering lay in reading the time lapse between a client request and an organizational response to that request. This was described with the formula $VT/TT = 1$ (value time/total time = 1). The tools with which to produce pure value time were characterized by investments in technology, job enlargement and flattening the rather long hierarchy in organizations (down sizing middle management). While reengineering was considered a "revolution" it did not substantially change the up down ideas about management roles delineated above, it simply enlarged the jobs of people that the manager was to coordinate and shortened the chain of command.[154]

Even in the healthcare management literature, the hierarchical function of the CEO is the object of emphasis: in two comparable evaluations of CEO functions in healthcare, one from the 1970s and the other from the 1990s the primary functions of the CEO are delineated as:[155]

- planning
- organizing
- controlling
- motivating
- coordinating

The field of organizational design introduced the concepts of project management and the matrix design. This seemed to go in the direction of recognizing the importance of horizontal integration. However, the matrix concept involves two figures: a generic management role responsible for the project and professional competence leaders responsible for the content. When matrix organizations and project managers were introduced in the organization they did not have the effect of favouring peer to peer integration. Instead, the employee of the matrix organization found him/herself in the extraordinarily complicated process of responding to two bosses, who did not respond to one another. So while the matrix organization and the project manager role seemed to be designed to forward horizontal integration in the organization, in practice a new line of authority on the basis of professional competence was added to the managerial line of authority with lots of confusion over who was the predominant figure of authority.

Healthcare management today, as described in the analysis provided in the previous chapters, has seen a paradigm shift in the management role from a predominantly vertical function to a horizontal one. The mere quantity of patients with needs that span as many as three and sometimes four different organizational pyramids serve to help visualize that the context must be visualized no longer as a pyramid but as wide plane. To help visualize this, today in the United States 1.6 million people are amputees. 80% of the amputations are due to disease. By 2050, the number of amputees in the United States is expected to triple (4.8 million people!). The needs of this group of amputees crosses professional boundaries and organizational ones: mobility, clinical issues like diabetes, obesity and cancer, as well as psychological and self-care issues.[156] The healthcare management context has been enlarged horizontally to include players that previously were excluded from the managerial "vision" of context, and has also repositioned roles that previously were thought to belong to the chain of command.

In examining the playing field of the manager, on the horizontal axis, new roles are emerging and established roles in healthcare management are experiencing a change of context. From the CEO, to the director of departments of primary care, to district managers and coordinators of integrated social and clinical services, managers are no longer asked to concentrate on the pyramid, but on the plane; these are peer to peer relationships. In the classical managerial paradigm of the pyramid, the manager is assigned authority over-resources, to determine and measure appropriate resource allocation. Today what most qualifies the manager is the capacity to prioritize and problem solve with other managers (peers) in different functions, and to pool resources with other organizations that most qualifies the healthcare management role. The playing field has become as wide as it is long.

As far as the healthcare professional's role in management is concerned, physicians too are facing the same change of context. Patients were previously treated by physicians and thought of in the vertical axis of the context. The very term "prescribe" a therapy literally means "to lay down a rule, to dictate". It was assumed that the patient would obey the command. However, patient compliance, which is defined as "conformity in fulfilling official requirements" has broken down: 50% of chronic patients over all age groups and diseases are known to be non-compliant.

That is, in not responding to authority, the patient is mutinous so to speak. The patient is no longer behaving as an obedient member of the hierarchical organization. In the few cases examined in the previous chapters where the role of the patient has been treated with a blended partnering relationship, health outcomes improve dramatically. Attempts to manage patient compliance with authority can be declared a failure based on the outcomes that have been observed. The "avoidable" costs of this non-compliance on the healthcare system have not been quantified but are staggering.

Therefore, the healthcare plane is not limited to professional and paid roles: physicians, nurses, administrative staff, etc, but includes the roles of patients and of their families. As the population ages and health problems become chronic, outcomes of healthcare organizations depend not only on the competence of the staff, but the cooperation of patients and families in achieving these outcomes. Patients and their families are a vital part of the organization. Families contain a wealth of information concerning patients' perceived health. Health status is on the one hand guaranteed by quality care, and on the other by compliance of the patient to treatment protocols.

The context in which the healthcare manager is acting is extended horizontally and includes new partners who were previously thought of as subordinates. The competence required to manage this context however is principally the capacity to integrate and organize a peer relationship. The peer to peer relationship has no embedded authority in it. It implies a capacity to collaborate. Managerial integration, both clinical and organizational, lies behind the concept of a network of services as much as behind a multi-disciplinary response.

The context has shifted from a cooperative to a non-cooperative game. The vertical authority system that used to define the healthcare management field has become obsolete as multi-dimensional health problems have increased in the population. Managerial horizontal integration is the managerial competence with which to respond to the issues presented in the non-cooperative game. Building a professional network is building a win-win solution in a non-cooperative game. That is, the manager must have the competence to work across departments (peer to peer) with patients and their families and with other organizations to build multi-disciplinary response systems, regardless of the like or dislike for the other people in the role. This requires specific expertise, in the understanding of the boundaries of the role itself, and how to build a peer to peer partnership. Today, nobody is thinking about this because the payoff or incentive is hidden. Managers and physicians cannot see that the optimal health and economic outcomes in healthcare will be a result of the partnership, not of individual strategies.

Peer to peer managers: leadership belongs to the group

The definition of role was discussed in the first chapter and highlighted three dimensions of the role: professional competence, relationship management, and respect for mutual role expectations. The principal competence that the peer to peer manager needs to possess is the ability to map technical expertise in the organization and to frame problems in such a way as to preserve role expectations. The boundaries between roles are given by the area of expertise of each role. In peer to peer integration a key to successful interaction is to frame objectives, share goals and criteria for measuring results, and to leave the solutions to the technical expertise involved.

Leadership has been amply described in the literature. In the vertical organization leadership refers to those individuals who are able to exercise influence over others without being influenced by others. In the literature, this has been described as "charismatic" leadership and people are thought to "be naturals" or not at this competence. In this kind of leadership the role of the boss and the leader is one and the same. In many profiles of CEOs, the journalist will report that the "CEO is a leader". The characteristic of the boss is that while he/she exercises authority, he/she also generates consensus. Observers of charismatic leaders have concluded that this kind of leadership is based on authority. This conclusion has been drawn not by observing the behaviour of the leader but by observing the behaviour of the "followers" or the members of the group. Group behaviour is consonant with principles of authority. When a group contains the boss, members of the group will behave according to the expectations of hierarchy: obedience. If there is a conflict in the group, members will expect the boss to resolve the conflict. If a group member expresses an idea, members of the group will expect the boss to decide whether or not the innovation should be implemented. In this version of leadership, a person assumes a personal style and mixes authority and style to influence others. In this context, a person may consider him/herself a leader. In simple terms Person = Leader.

In the peer group, leadership by contrast, does not belong to individual members, but is a tool for the group. This type of leadership is known as situational leadership.[157] It distinguishes leadership as authority from leadership as recognition. In the peer group or situation of horizontal integration, leadership is not imposed but it is recognized by the others. A member of the group cannot decide to exercise leadership, it is the other members of the group that attribute leadership. In simple terms, the group decides who the leader is, it is not the leader who decides who the leader is. In order to exercise this type of leadership, the group must be a peer group and cannot contain hierarchical roles. The behaviour of members of the group, in the absence of authority, changes towards issues like resolving conflicts or forwarding an idea. In a peer group, conflict is a problem that belongs to the group to solve. If a member has an idea, he/she will forward the idea. If the group refuses the idea, the member will not give up, or succumb to the authority of peers, he/she will work on the sidelines to create alliances. These alliances are temporary and depend on the issue being discussed. In the absence of authority, the behaviour of group members towards certain issues changes. Group members assume different behaviours than they would in the presence of authority. In this context, effectiveness revolves around framing the problem at a level that is non-invasive for the individual members of the group, and negotiating alliances to promote ideas.

The problem is that situational leadership is not a natural phenomenon, but needs to be taught. Condo owners in a building should theoretically adapt a situational leadership model, but as anyone who has been a condominium owner can affirm, this simply does not happen. Peer to peer relationship skills can be learned and this will be the subject of the rest of this chapter.

In the theory of situational leadership, leadership is a function that every member of the group can assume according to the expertise that is required, according to group members. This can be technical competence in some cases, but in many cases it is relationship competence: a sense of humour, a passionate discourse, a logical interpretation, etc.

Healthcare management is identifying the peer group as the principal site of the healthcare management function. For a CEO of a local health authority, the group that will define the multi-disciplinary response may involve the CEO of the hospital, the CEO of the local authority and the CEO of the larger non-profit organization. For directors of departments it is their capacity to work horizontally that characterizes this role. In this context leadership is a function of the group, and according to the objective that the group is facing, leadership will alternate, because recognition will move from one actor to another.

Peer to peer relationship management: developing an appropriate expectation

Healthcare managers, in developing peer to peer relationship competence, must come to terms with the limits of authority. Authority and charismatic leadership can be exercised within the organization and the department on the hierarchical axis. On the other hand, peer situations are situations in which recognition of the others determines leadership. The use of authority in peer situations generates disastrous outcomes as described in the following example.

The Evil Eye

A 35-year old man from the Ivory Coast living in Italy, a metal worker by profession, of the Muslim religion, with a history of working regularly, living autonomously in an apartment, of having a social life, turned to the Office of Services for Immigrants asking for help. He claimed he was a victim of the evil eye put on him by his father. He was the only son of his father's second wife, and was the "prince of the household" until his father's first wife, who had appeared unable to have children, had a son. He was then sent away from home and faced many hardships. Years later he married a woman he loved and had a son. He came to Italy to provide for them. While he was gone, his wife was accused of having an affair with another man. His father forced him to repudiate her even if he did not want to. Very unhappy, a couple of years later, he reconciled with his wife, against his father's wishes. His father then launched "the evil eye". Since his father had done this to him, he had been unable to sleep and was convinced that people were out to "get him".

Shortly thereafter, after a street fight, he was arrested by the police, and was examined by a psychiatrist who diagnosed the

The Evil Eye – *continued*

patient with paranoid schizophrenia and orders "involuntary patient commitment" He is hospitalized and placed on anti-psychotic medication. After leaving the hospital, he loses his job as the medication makes him slow, he finishes his savings and is placed into a managed home. Some of the case workers in the health authority who have been exposed to cultural diversity issues are concerned about this man. They ask for my specialized intervention as I am a psychologist, expert in cultural diversity.

In six sessions, we work within his cultural frame on freeing him from the evil eye that his father has sent him, he feels much better and he asks to be taken off his medication because it is impeding him from holding a job and reacquiring a normal life. I arrange to meet the psychiatrist to discuss the case.

At the meeting, I explain the culture of the evil eye, I reread the series of unfortunate events that the man from the Ivory Coast has recounted, and explain the six sessions and the results of my intervention. Lastly I request that he be taken off medication on the basis that he has been misdiagnosed in that there has not been a proper cultural frame in reading his clinical history.

The psychiatrist refuses to reevaluate his reading of the case. He refuses to stop medication and curtly informs me that a paranoid schizophrenic cannot be taken off medication.[158]

This is an example of a peer to peer relationship in the absence of a third party, and the difficulty of making this relationship work. The intercultural psychologist is well-informed and is probably also right, the patient is probably not schizophrenic. However, this is the content of the communication. In the proposed relationship with a peer, she has not recognized the limits of authority: she cannot force the psychiatrist to do something. She does not hold authority over the psychiatrist. What can be observed in the example is that the psychologist tells the psychiatrist what to do next. Instead of respecting the peer to peer nature of the relationship, she develops an expectation that the psychiatrist should do what she says. The psychiatrist, regardless of the right and wrong thing to do for the patient, becomes infuriated with the psychologist for not respecting the peer to peer nature of their relationship. He refuses the relationship with her all together, even though this ultimately damages the patient. The role expectation that the psychiatrist had coming into the relationship was violated, and this is a fatal error in the peer to peer relationship.

A correct frame for a peer to peer relationship cannot be that one actor tells the other what to do. To use authority is to assault the role expectation of a peer. Every member of the organization holds the expectation that his/her technical expertise will be recognized. If the psychiatrist does what the psychologist tells him to do, he is giving up his peer relationship status and succumbing to the authority of the psychologist, and to all intents and purposes if he obeys he becomes a subordinate to the psychologist.

In a peer to peer relationship a reasonable expectation is characterized by a request to reevaluate a situation. Reevaluation does not necessarily guarantee the desired outcome. While a desired outcome can be an appropriate expectation for a boss towards a subordinate, it is an inappropriate expectation in a peer to peer relationship. Ideally, in the case of the evil eye, the cultural diversity expert would have read the situation from her perspective and then asked the psychiatrist to read his view, and they would have worked together to frame an appropriate response to the situation.

Keeping the peer to peer nature of the relationship as the top priority in managing the case is a more promising road to doing something constructive for the patient then pushing the desired outcome onto a peer, thus destroying the peer to peer relationship between the caregivers.

Too often, especially in healthcare, where a "case is at heart", peer to peer integration between professionals becomes a battle of authority. The consequence is, as can be seen in this case, that the relationship breaks down. Therefore, in peer to peer partnerships, role boundaries are defined by a frame of the problem that must be mutually inclusive. Solutions cannot be imposed with authority, regardless of whether there may indeed be a "right" and a "wrong". The frame and the capacity to see the balance of the peer to peer relationship as the solution to the problem is professional expertise.

Rational choice is a common language for developing peer to peer relationships

While when acting in the hierarchy of the organization an authority figure can make decisions on the basis of opinions, in peer to peer relationships opinions weaken the meaning of the peer to peer relationships themselves. If managers do not turn to rational choice models to inform their contributions, but generalize based on professional experience, they will communicate "opinions" rather than "information" to one another. While in a hierarchy opinions and generalizations survive because authority saves them, in a peer structure opinions destroy the peer to peer integration between players. In general, introducing opinions or generalizations into the peer relationship structure is a sneaky way of introducing authority into a partnership and it destroys the efficacy of the peer group itself. Opinions do not favour peer to peer integration.

This is not easy to learn because experience with hierarchy teaches the opposite: opinions = decisions. For example, legislation banning certain kinds of dogs or requiring them to be muzzled, in all countries is almost always passed by the equivalent of the minister of health following an attack on a human being, especially a small child. Statistical analysis demonstrates that breeds of dog are not connected to dogs biting humans. It is the owner's aggressiveness and mistreatment that makes for an aggressive dog regardless of breed. A couple of cases of pit bulls attacking children can lead to massive legislation. However, the reason two pit bulls in a row were involved is simply due to the popularity of the breed among aggressive and sadistic owners. Legislation that bans certain breeds, or that muzzles certain breeds, has not been informed by statistical analysis but by recent experience, and decision making based on opinion is not effective.[159] In fact, dog bites will continue to occur, only they will involve other kinds of dogs.

Managers, clinicians, professionals, and policy makers often "generalize" from their experience. These generalizations are only opinions. They have no scientific premises. However, hierarchy allows opinions and generalizations to survive. Often those managerial decisions that do work lead us to believe that some people are better "opinion leaders" than others. On the other hand, it is impossible to create meaningful peer to peer integration on the basis of generalizations or extrapolation from experience: people in peer to peer relationships cannot weigh opinions because the nature of the peer group implies an equal weight for the opinion of each member.

One particularly amusing example of the inefficacy of opinions based on experience and generalizations in the peer group is captured in the list of 43 characteristics that US drug enforcement agents compiled to catch drug smugglers based on their experience. Each of these characteristics has equal weight, yet the absurdity of compiling opinions in the peer group can be shown by looking at them all together. Nineteen of the 43 ways to catch a drug dealer coming off an airplane according to drug enforcement agents are listed here:

"Arrived late at night; arrived early in the morning; arrived in afternoon; one of the first to deplane; one of the last to deplane, deplaned in the middle, purchased ticket at the airport, made reservation on short notice, bought coach ticket, bought first class ticket, used one way ticket, used round trip ticket…carried no luggage, carried brand new luggage, carried a small bag, carried a medium sized bag, carried two bulky garment bags, carried two heavy suitcases, carried four pieces of luggage…"[160]

The data observed are inherently unstable. That is, a drug smuggler can arrive and deplane anytime, with a one way or a round trip ticket and any kind of luggage. These generalizations of "successful apprehensions" are not useful for predicting future behaviour or for directing future apprehensions because they are based on unstable behaviour on the one hand, and are generalizations from personal experience on the other. There is nothing systematic about this frame. This is a compilation of opinions that does nothing to forward the apprehension of drug smugglers. Paradoxically, how to catch a drug smuggler is weakened not strengthened by this peer group effort.

While hierarchy facilitates generalizations and opinions by sustaining them with authority, peer to peer relationships have to function on the basis of mutual recognition and cannot function effectively on arbitrary content. In order to foster this relationship a scientific compilation of information is necessary.

Where rational choice models have been used to create a common language with which to build networks, generalizations can be avoided. "Many of the most convincing success stories told to us by ex-students involve the use of concepts from our (rational choice) courses to clarify and communicate during collaborative decision making".[161] In fact, while clinicians are convinced of the importance of their own past experience in informing choices and utilizing resources, statistical studies have demonstrated that their capacities are poorer than a statistical model.

Rational choice models and intuitive management require the collection and analysis of data according to scientific method and the laws of probability. In the healthcare management role, the application of rational choice and intuitive management applies not only to "hard data", financial, utilization, personnel, but also is a necessary tool for analysing non-verbal communication. Various studies have suggested that only 15% of human communication is based on verbal exchange. The rest depends on the non-verbal, facial expressions, body language, tone, rhythm and volume of voice. A physician who is shuffling papers on the desk, taking calls and typing at the computer while relaying a diagnosis communicates more disinterest in the patient than the elements of the diagnosis that are the verbal object of the exchange.

Rational choice models must be informed not only by financial information, utilization data, and clinical data, but by non-verbal and verbal clues as to the health of relationships within the organization. The healthcare manager must have an excellent understanding of the laws of probability but also a sensitivity towards collecting and reading "non-traditional" forms of information in the communication process.

Malpractice litigation and hidden literacy problems for example, are often expressed indirectly and non-verbally but cost the health system about US $200 billion a year in the United States. Illiteracy is always expressed indirectly or not at all. "Excuse me doctor I forgot my glasses, could you read me the prescription", is an example.

The content of non-verbal and indirect verbal clues to thin slice and identify these issues is critical. Little has been done in terms of developing rational choice models for modelling and interpreting this non-verbal data that emerge from patients and their families.

Applying rational choice models to healthcare management could have some significant effects on costs, not only in reducing litigation with patients but also in the costs of staffing services. For example, rational choice models have demonstrated that in the clinical field of psychology, effectiveness of psychotherapy is independent of professional preparation and licensing. That is, psychotherapy works, but patients in therapy get better to the same degree with highly trained professionals as they do with barely trained professionals. It would seem that psychotherapy does produce results, but these depend more on a regression phenomenon of patient status than on the training of the professional. That is, the patient turns to the therapist when he/she is extremely unhappy. In the lives of most people there are extremely happy moments, and extremely unhappy moments. Each of these moments tend to dissolve into moments that are neither one nor the other. Therefore the work of psychotherapists does not depend on the tools that they use, or their level of preparation, but on the natural regression cycle of the patient towards less emotionally charged moments. Only statistical models with control groups can determine the effectiveness of treatment, on the one hand, and on the other, an adequate professional profile and reasonable fee for the service provided.[162]

Healthcare management is faced with the challenge of reducing the "avoidable" costs of the system and this depends on sharpening the rational choice model as a tool for managing peer to peer relationships, with patients and with other professionals inside and outside the organization. The rational choice model and probability theory represent a language with which peers can share and discuss information in the absence of authority. Therefore, knowledge of the rational choice model and probability are quintessential for the preparation of the healthcare manager in the new context.

Blended peer to peer relationships: trust and rational choice

The trust model suggests that both interpersonal trust and rational choice inform and strengthen the organization. The management system is asked to manage risks that various actors are reciprocally undertaking towards one another. This requires attentive management of the interests of the actors involved and of sharing risk.

Rational choice can become a common language between peers in the professional context, it limits opinions and attempts at assuming authority by insisting on the evidence, and is therefore fundamental to the peer to peer relationship. In the partnership with patients, the knowledge base of rational choice needs to inform decisions but the interpersonal trust relationship needs to be there too, in a word, a blended relationship.

The physician is a manager of the patients who are part of the organization even though they are not salaried. Each physician manages thousands of patients a year. So while the physician may not be a manager in the traditional sense of the term, he/she manages patients who are the beneficiaries of the organizational process. As chronic illness has increased, the patient has to look after him/herself most of the time: diet, exercise, smoking cessation, and looking for symptoms like weight gain or loss, are the critical ingredients for maintaining health status in chronic situations. Patients have become as responsible as the physician for a positive outcome of the care process.

In the absence of managerial trust, that is, trust in the organization on the part of the patient, the patient organizes his/her own caretakers by negotiating with each clinician individually. This means that the management function is suffering from ineffective peer to peer relationships from the clinical to the organizational level. This peer to peer relationship void leaves the management function in the hands of the patient him/herself rather than in the hands of the organization.

When the patient experiences or perceives difficulties in the organizational system, he/she begins a long search for the right person. In terms of the interpersonal trust structure, the healthcare organization today is characterized by the importance of the person inside the role. While organizational theory imagines the role as independent of the person, the healthcare organization has an important personalization of the role. This personalization has influenced healthcare organizations both in public and in private systems.

So while management might be organizing a systematic response, the perception of the patient is that what counts is the person who helps you, and the organization does not in fact give systematic responses but personal ones. Emblematic of how the personal relationship system has destroyed the managerial function is given by an Italian LHA. The prenatal care call centre for making prenatal appointments had a waiting list that was nine months long. So the system is actively declaring to the patient that "there must be a better way" to obtain prenatal care then turning to the organization.

Malpractice indicates that the patient looks for blended relationships. This is specific to the healthcare sector. Patients will sue on the basis of their perceptions of the physician communication and not on the basis of the medical error.

The QoL research showed the limits of well-intentioned physicians who rely exclusively on clinical data, or on rational choice and probability, to guarantee treatment to cancer patients over-listening to subjective quantifications of QoL. Without a personalization of this scientific knowledge, perceived efficacy of treatment is low. As clinicians have been encouraged to rely more on scientific research and less on arbitrary decision making, they have abandoned the relationship with the patient. There needs to be a balance between trust and rational choice.

For the physician, the relationship with the patient is a vehicle for applying scientific discovery to benefit the patient community. Therefore while the introduction of clinical protocols has corrected arbitrary treatment decisions and increased the quality and appropriateness of care, the benefits of rational choice have not been widely perceived, as treatment is not delivered with special attention to the person in the relationship. Each patient needs to be heard as an individual with a lifestyle, habits and hobbies and treatment needs to be placed into the container of the patient's life.

Blended relationships and professional discretion lie in managing the perception of treatment just as much as the delivery of treatment. The data shows that patients need to talk, they talk to their families who have no skills or tools for responding. The study of cystic fibrosis management in the most successful hospital in the United States evidenced that the physician worked with the perception of the patient, first of all in sharing information that the patient was non-compliant and then in developing an acceptable blended relationship that would allow her to comply. The physician is responsible for managing the rational choice process of identifying the care path and for managing the perceptions of patients and families into blended relationships.

Diversity issues

Professional discretion applies not only to the relationship between physicians, patients and their families, but also applies to the relationship between physicians. A peer to peer core competence is the capacity to focus on the perception of the "other" in the relationship rather than on the "intentions" with which the relationship is proposed. The definition of intention is "a determination to act in a certain way"[163] and perception is "what can be discerned by the senses".[164] Therefore, intention is about "what I meant to say", and perception is about "how I felt when you said it". Intentions are often born of assumptions, the "supposition that something is true".

The issue of perception and intention can seem a sociological question, and can hardly be visualized as a managerial competence. These issues have instead been at the forefront of managerial competence with all employers in the United States over the last decade. Perception and intention entered the managerial profile in the hierarchy, under the heading "diversity management".

The issue of perception and intention is embedded in the healthcare field because of this field's exposure to cultural diversity, both inside the workplace and with patients. Managing diversity has been analysed extensively in the pyramid and hardly applied to peer to peer relationships. In any case, the historical rise of this issue to a workplace managerial question renders the idea of introducing it in peer to peer relationships less obscure.

Inside the organization in industrialized countries, certain professions have seen a lack of qualified resources on the job market, specifically in the nursing profession. In European countries the most diverse cultural workforce in public administration can be found in nursing. In the United States diversity is a labour relations issue as much as a service dimension. This is becoming true in Europe too, where immigration patterns have affected the typical student in schools and also have had a strong impact on healthcare, putting organizations in a position where they must react to different ideas of health, care, and even physician-patient communication.

Historically the issues of diversity management began with women in the workplace, known by the slogan "equal work, equal pay". However, the issues of compensation were only the beginning of the impact of diversity on the workplace. Another dimension that has received full legal recognition is the workplace as a context, and therefore as an area not only for compensation inequity but of organizational climate and its psychological effect on employees' health and their careers.

The issue is that a "hostile" work environment can affect an employee's performance, health and career opportunity regardless of compensation, potential, intelligence and qualification. The Equal Employment Opportunity Commission, a federal agency, interprets the Civil Rights Act of 1964 known as Title VII: "Title VII prohibits not only intentional discrimination, but also practices that have the effect of discriminating against individuals because of their race, color, national origin, religion, or sex".[165] Title VII also prohibits sex discrimination and introduces the concept of "hostile environment": "workplace conditions that create a hostile environment for persons of either gender". The hostile environment standard also applies "on the bases of race, color, national origin, religion, age and disability".[166]

What was recognized in this legislation was the right of a minority to declare a "perceived" hostility, regardless of the intentions of management or the organization. The issue of perception and intention really frames the issue of diversity management and allows for a better understanding of many changes that have been brought to the management of the workplace.

Racism, like the issues concerning women, is defined as an "institutionalized system of economic, political, social and cultural relations that ensures that one racial group has and maintains power and privilege over all others". Again, in defining racism, intentions are thought to be inconsequential "Individual participation in racism occurs when the objective outcome of behaviour reinforces these relations, regardless of the subjective intent".[167]

In 1976, Ryan published an important book that showed how the process of racial integration was in fact positioned in good intentions but was preserving the institutionalized system.[168] The process of racial integration which included quotas in colleges and affirmative action in the workplace according to Ryan's interpretation was a strategy that Ryan called "Blame the Victim". Blaming the victim was a position that looked for the origins of problems in the victims rather than asking how they became victims. Its resolution was to create the conditions for effecting change in the "victim population" to make them more like the dominant one. His work reread affirmative action and quotas to mean: take a certain number of victims and place them in virtuous conditions so that they can learn to behave like us.

Diversity in the workplace in this philosophical frame can be understood as deviation from a norm. What can we do to make them more like us? This understanding of diversity has done nothing to reduce costly litigation and ethical issues of inequity.

An example of "blame the victim" mentality occurred recently (1999)[169] in Italy in a very famous rape case. The woman who had been raped was accused by the defendant of having worn tight jeans. His defence went on to explain that her jeans were so tight, that only she could have helped him take them off. The defendant was declared innocent by the Supreme Court on the reasoning that the jeans were impossible to remove. "It is impossible to take off jeans...without the active cooperation of the person who is wearing them"[170] and the court concluded that therefore the event had been consensual. This case received international attention and was nicknamed "the denim defence". Marches against the denim defence were held around the world, and the term is still used ironically to describe "blame the victim" injustices by women struggling to obtain legal recognition of their rights in their countries.

What the denim defence hides is the institutional assumption that a woman wearing tight clothes "wants sex". In rape trials in the United States as in later formulations of "hostile environments" it was conceded that in order to draw attention towards social and institutional hostility, the perception of the victim would take precedence over the intention of the "perpetrator". There would be no more blame the victim. Perception was deemed determining whether or not the perpetrator, be it an organization or a manager or another employee, a husband or a date intended to harm. From cases like these, the precedent emerged for the perception of the victim to override the intention of the defendant. This led to the concept of crimes that prior to this time had not existed, as such: date-rape and also rape inside the confines of a legal marriage and common home.

In the United States, the idea of the driving point of a case being in perception and not intention, puts the burden of creating a non-hostile working environment on management and on every employee in the organization. It recognizes that a dominant culture is not aware of its minority counterpart's sensitivity and imposes on that dominant culture an attentive examination of its assumptions, most of which must be overturned in order to effectively manage a diverse workforce or clients. In other words, the denim defence hides institutional assumptions about women's clothing and their sexual availability. By moving away from blaming the victim as a philosophy, the issue became to uncover the causes and not the effects.

In the healthcare management context, this is also the case. Management control has proven that one of the major costs of the system are GPs' prescriptions to their patients. In Italy, there was so much variability in prescription practices over a statistically adjusted patient population that a budget mechanism was introduced to standardize care paths and reduce pharmacological spending among GPs. Monetary incentives were connected to targets. Attentive analysis of the data shows that physicians prescribe according to their regular patterns up until the last trimester. In the last trimester they drastically reduce prescriptions. It is evident that their perception of the problem is that they are the "blamed victims" of cost reduction, and inconsistent and ineffective care practices have increased rather than decreased. Management intention to offer clinical protocols was obscured by physician perception that managers just don't want to spend money.

Workplace managers were concerned. How can we know what we are assuming if we are assuming it? Workplace efforts to integrate diversity, actions like affirmative action were being understood as "blame the victim". The United States, at a state and a federal level, has recognized the right to equal employment opportunity for workers belonging to different races, sexes, age, cultures, religions and in a few states of sexual orientation. If a worker perceived an offence, it was his perception that informed the offence. Whether or not management had intentionally undermined his integrity was not at issue. This is born logically from the concept of equal treatment. If all workers are to be given equal employment opportunity, and if cultural assumptions wind up creating disparity, it is the right of the worker to feel treated equally. It is the prerogative of management to challenge assumptions that might damage that perception. The management of diversity in the workplace needed to be understood by management as it is defined in biology as "bio diversity" where it is intended as a rich variety. The tendency of managers was to focus solutions on how to fix the victim rather than on how to fix the production of victims.

As can be seen, in recognizing the diverse workforce, issues of management have been strongly impacted. Furthermore, given that "good intentions" or "cultural assumptions" were worth nothing in a court case, organizations had to create sensitivity in the workforce and in management in general to the "grey area" of "acceptable behaviour" in order to determine correct working relationships. The need to know what not to assume was huge.

In the United States, where the legal problems of diversity management have forced organizations to try to act, the intention-perception problem has been treated with an approach known as "politically correct" which has been berated for its superficiality in many different literary works (Oleanna, The Human Stain). A new language was born that sought to eliminate "assumptions" of any kind from the workplace vocabulary and workplace behaviour. This involved the production of procedures and manuals which describe how men and women should talk to one another in the organization, and a new language called "politically correct" that involves a non-historical non-judgemental identification of diversity. It tries to take assumptions out of the language.

Its critics claim that it takes intelligence out of relationships. Since only 15% of communication is in fact transmitted verbally, changing words does not change perceptions.

Some examples of this new "politically correct language" include "differently able" instead of "handicapped" or "disabled". The words "handicapped" and "disabled" immediately drew attention to what the person was missing, while "differently able" highlighted the fact that there was a difference but that enabled. "Native American" instead of "Indian". The term "Indian" evoked the cowboys and Indians, and the practice of scalping or other negative or stereotypical imagery. The word "Native American", simply denotes that the population was native to the United States. Lastly, "downsized" or "early retirement" instead of "fired or laid off". This new terminology wished to detach the situation of the worker from the stereotypical implications of using the previous term. For example, being "fired" had the stigma of not having been an effective performer or being old. Being "downsized" referred to a corporate need to reduce the workforce and did not have personal implications and "early retirement" seemed a rejuvenating choice rather than a stamp that read "used up". The use of the word "gay" among men to affirm homosexual masculine bonding had to go, jokes of a sexual nature were prohibited as they could be perceived as offensive to women.

This has been made fun of in literary and academic circles nationally and internationally, though in the United States it has become a manual of workplace etiquette.

The diversity management issue, which in simple terms is an issue of perceptions assuming priority over-intentions and assumptions, is an ongoing process in the vertical field of management. The same "good intentions" inform horizontal relationships in the healthcare organization. In fact, today peer to peer relationships function in feeling relationships, that is where good intentions match good perceptions. Where this does not happen, the peer to peer relationship, regardless of the importance of this relationship to reaching organizational outcomes, tends to cause closure and "abandonment" of the relationship itself. This puts emphasis on the person over the role. The result is the creation of feeling networks that structurally ignore roles, procedures and systemic responses. The healthcare manager requires an attention to perception rather than to intention at all levels.

Applied to the specificity of the healthcare environment, the perception-intention expertise is necessary to develop blended relationships in the peer group.

Peer to peer relationship management: aligning perceptions regardless of intentions

In the public system, in Italy for example, relationships between people determine the speed of transactions and the use of resources. The feeling relationships in the organization are characterized by the simple function intention = perception. Where there is feeling, there is no work to do for the proposed relationship because feeling relationships can be described as those relationships where intention = perception. Where these relationships exist people in the organization utilize resources to resolve problems in the here and now, and override roles and procedures put into place to guarantee systematic responses and appropriateness. Intentions and perceptions of the players are aligned.

Building horizontal integration in the organization is hard work. In fact, peer to peer relationships are hard work. While marriages are peer to peer relationships but start with feeling, and the free choice to make the marriage a contract, peer to peer blended relationships have to happen between people who may not have chosen to have anything to do with one another if given a choice.

The result is that feeling networks handle the problems they face with the people that understand one another. However, feeling is not universal, and often intention does not correspond to perception. The primary proposed relationship competence that the manager must possess to create this network response system is to put the emphasis on the perception of communication rather than on the intention of the communication.

The following example of an interpersonal conflict from a University classroom helps to focus the important issue of intentions as cultural assumptions (and this applies in general to any culture including organizational and small groups) and the importance of prioritizing perception over-intention in the peer to peer relationship.

The students were enrolled in a Masters program in International Healthcare management. There were 30 students from 21 countries. Among these students were a Palestinian male who had never left Palestine, and a Spanish male who had been 20 years in the scout movement. Both were between 25–30.

The Palestinian was married and came to Europe to study, and in order to get to Italy passed through Egypt. It was his first time out of his country. In Egypt he was arrested, his documents were confiscated, and for three days he sat in a prison cell isolated and without information. Finally, he was given back his documents and allowed to transit to Europe. Naturally, his first outing from home and family had not been easy.

The Spanish student, true to the scouting tradition, was an integrator in the internationally diverse classroom. He organized multi-ethnic dinners and was very careful to include everyone. He was also extremely attentive to women: he always opened doors, helped with the coat, the chair, and noticed and complimented a new piece of clothing or a haircut.

One day, the Palestinian came to class dressed in a suit and a tie and having had a shave. He had an appointment with a professor and his tradition required this type of dress for a meeting with a professor. The Spanish student immediately noticed his elegance and made the following comment: "you look so sharp today, I am sure all the girls will go crazy for you".

The Palestinian's face froze, but he did not say anything.

The Palestinian student avoided the Spanish student all day. The Spanish student assumed he was in a bad mood.

After avoiding the Spanish student all day, the Palestinian stopped the Spanish student as they were leaving class and asked him for a word in private. He said "don't you dare speak to me that way again". The Spanish student was flabbergasted. He apologized but begged to be informed as to what he could have done wrong.

The Palestinian student explained "I am a married man and a religious person, to tell me IN FRONT OF THE WHOLE CLASS that the girls will go crazy for me is an insult to my integrity".

This is an interesting case, because though the Spanish student has extensive scouting experience, and considers himself an expert in managing relationships of all kinds, his assumption that a man will always feel complimented if told that the women will go crazy for him is so "obvious", so assumed from his cultural background that even when the Palestinian sends him non-verbal and verbal messages of how offensive he had been – the Spanish student is unable to "see" his gaffe until it is literally spelled out for him. His assumptions underlie his good intentions, and therefore he is blind to the clues that he has created a negative perception. The Palestinian, despite the fact that he perceived an offence, did challenge the assumptions and intentions of the Spanish student. It is the capacity to express perceptions on the one hand, and adjust assumptions on the other, that enable a professional to develop a functional peer to peer blended relationship and network. In fact, in this case the two students were able to construct a lasting professional relationship despite the differences in their personal views and assumptions. They each possessed the ability to look at perceptions and give them a qualifying role over-assumptions and intentions. In communication theory this is known as the competence to consider punctuation.

The question of intentions and perceptions is aptly described by communication theory as a punctuation problem in the proposed relationship. The proposed relationship is not the content of the communication; it is the instructions concerning that content. In human communication, "I am just joking" is an example of the importance of the proposed relationship in interpreting or making use of the content. Communication theory isolates a concept of cause and effect, and observes that there may not be shared views as to who is providing the cause and who is suffering the effect. "Disagreement about how to punctuate the sequence of events is at the root of countless relationship struggles".[171] The following example of a budget communication is emblematic. The LHA found that not all pregnancies were being followed in pre-natal care. Thus they formulated the budget objective for districts that read: "increase the number of pregnancies in pre-natal care". The District Manager, exasperated, commented "how can I be expected to make them get pregnant?" and concluded that whoever was managing the organization knew nothing about healthcare. Clearly, both context and punctuation has contributed to this relationship struggle.

Another example, of a husband and a wife who find themselves in a negative pattern of behaviour, further illustrates the concept of punctuation in a proposed relationship.

> The wife claims that the husband is withdrawn and will not talk. The husband claims that the wife is constantly nagging. Neither denies the behaviour that the other accuses him/her of, although each frame his/her own behaviour as he/she intended it. In fact, he denies that he is withdrawing but affirms that he is "getting some personal space", and she denies that she is nagging but claims that she is "helping him to talk". In looking more closely at each one's position, each is reading the situation from his intention and not from the others' perception of the behaviour.
>
> The husband sees the sequence: she nags, I look for personal space, she nags, I look for personal space, etc.
>
> The wife sees the sequence: He withdraws, I help him talk, he withdraws, I help him talk.

This is called the punctuation of an interaction. The husband and wife are punctuating the interaction based on their respective intentions. Neither is putting emphasis on the perception of the other, regardless of their intentions.

Let us take the example of the Palestinian and the Spanish student.

The Spanish student sees the sequence: I make a compliment, he is in a bad mood.

The Palestinian student sees the sequence: I am in a good mood, he insults me and pretends nothing has happened.

In their clarification they were able to arrive at a common punctuation:

Spanish student:
I made a misunderstood compliment that was not in good taste, he told me what I had done. We can talk.
Palestinian student:
He made an assumption that he was not aware of, I told him, he apologized. We can talk.

The important competence is that the last affirmation of the sequence is shared by both members of the proposed relationship. It is the ability to discuss perceptions, reframe assumptions and marginalize intentions that is the core relationship competence necessary to correct a punctuation problem. Punctuation problems are the most common problem in building peer to peer integration between roles. The frame perception, intention and assumption can be used to reread the considerations developed in the previous chapters.

This punctuation problem often causes the two subjects to simply abandon the proposed relationship and defend themselves one from the other. Organizational roles, procedures and processes are used to block the proposed relationship and any information it may carry.

Successful cases of blended relationships in the healthcare sector have shown that this particular environment could benefit from a mediation between personal relationships and roles, termed "blended relationship" or "professional discretion". These relationships are characterized by the ability to talk about punctuation and to arrive at a shared punctuation on the basis of the autonomy granted by the role. For example, in the case of cystic fibrosis management, the physician who could look at the perception of his good clinical intentions, and discuss the punctuation of the relationship was able to change the relationship from a noncompliant to a compliant relationship with his patient. This applies to both organizational management and clinical management.

While this has long been considered a problem of communication, it has been demonstrated in the previous chapters that this is to some extent a problem of interpersonal communication but in equal measure a challenge of how to organize services. The organization can be a tool for creating mutual punctuation in the proposed relationship. The example of the difficulty of creating shared punctuation between mothers and nurses over-breastfeeding is emblematic. Nurses felt that they were communicating the importance of breastfeeding and mothers were feeling the frustration of breastfeeding. By using the organization to punctuate the relationship between mother and newborn baby through the "rooming-in" system, it has been demonstrated that organization can be used to share punctuation in the relationship between nurses, mothers and newborns.

In conclusion, the healthcare managerial expertise can be defined as follows:

- an understanding of the limits of authority and the need for horizontal managerial action
- an understanding of role expertise and boundaries between peer roles
- a frame of trust with which to manage partnerships, that is a rigorous preparation in rational choice models and probability theory on the one hand, and an understanding of how professional discretion, that is the capacity to discuss perceptions regardless of intentions, plays into building interpersonal trust.

7
Conclusions: Management Education

Introduction

As the population lives longer patients need to receive multi-disciplinary responses. If the organization is unable to build peer to peer relationships, patients are managing their own care. One out of two chronic patients is non-compliant. This is detrimental to providing appropriate care and to controlling its costs. The greatest opportunities for healthcare managers lie in making existent services appropriate, of high quality, and cost effective.

The previous chapters have sought to make a case for the ample and untapped opportunities for health systems to provide more appropriate, higher quality care at lower costs without having to resort to cutting or curtailing the health services provided. Many unnecessary costs of the system are connected to quite a primitive relationship management model that only contemplates hierarchical relationships. At least 20% and perhaps as much as 35% of the costs of the US health system are "avoidable" and they almost always have to do with relationship management issues. The opportunities for blended peer to peer relationships appear to be first and foremost within and between healthcare organizations and then with the patient.

The previous chapters have established the need to make this cultural breakthrough, and the question is how to cultivate and distribute expertise. This chapter is dedicated to proposing some ideas on how schools of management can encourage students to develop peer to peer relationship skills for healthcare management careers while they are in the classroom.

Schools of scientific rigour and schools of practice

Students of schools of management tend to enrol in one of three types of management development experiences; full time and part time degree programs, executive education catalogue certificate courses and finally tailor designed executive education courses for a specific organization. These last products are known as "bespoke" programs. This comes from 17th century London tailors from Saville Row whose customers would choose the length of cloth they desired for their clothing and this piece of cloth would be "bespoke" which stood for "be spoken for". It is used to describe executive programs where programs are "made to measure for the client". They are unique to the organization and generally include client case material and presentations to senior management.

2005 and 2006 have seen a "self-critique" of the efficacy of these products by two leading institutions in Europe and in the United States. A 2006 study by the Oxford Said Business School revealed that both public and private organizations in Great Britain are spending up to "75 million pounds" on executive education courses that according to the results of the research are a big waste of money. The school defines the criteria for a quality executive program: "The programme should address the right issue in the first place; it should be tailored precisely to the needs of the commissioning organization; and its success (or otherwise) should be properly evaluated. Our (Oxford) report suggests that most organizations are failing in at least one, if not all three of these respects".[172] The data from the report queries 500 executives and HR directors, and finds that only 35% of HR directors and 21% of executives found that organizational development strategy was meeting organizational objectives.[173]

In an equally charged Harvard Business Review article entitled "Where business schools lost their way", another critique focuses on how schools of management do not produce managers in the organization.

This extremely recent debate on management research and education identifies a struggle between two schools of thought which can be described simply as the school of scientific rigour on the one hand, and the school of practice on the other. The history of the school of management gives insight into this very current debate.

The school of management was once a trade school taught by foremen, factory managers and other managers in the field. It was a school where practitioners told their story to other practitioners. In the 1950s major and influential foundations like the Ford and Carnegie Foundations criticized the trade school approach of the business school and recommended a more scientific approach to business issues.[174] The argument was that it was quite simply uninteresting to describe single business environments and solutions. Making the parallel to medicine it was akin to a physician publishing an article about how he/she found and treated a rash in a patient "that he/she had never seen before". Scientific methods were necessary to observe and classify on the one hand and to treat problems of growth and managerial sustainability on the other.

Nearly 60 years later, the result of this invitation to become more scientifically rigorous is that business schools encourage their professors to pursue what are considered "academic standards". Professors are expected to measure themselves against the scientific standard in academia. Careers in business schools and schools of management are evaluated on the basis of scientific contribution to research and visibility through publication.

However, the questions posed in this vast body of research are often of little interest to the practitioner. "The system creates pressure on scholars to publish articles on narrow subjects chiefly of interest to other academics, not practitioners".[175] Put in simple terms in order to answer a question using scientific methods, the question has to be reduced to one that you can answer in those terms, and then it may often turn out to be of little or no interest to have answered it.

To remain within the conceptual frame of this book, scientific rigour and practice can be seen as necessary and equally weighted issues. In reality there is a non-cooperative game between rigour and practice and the optimal outcome of this non-cooperative game is relevance. The definition of relevant is "having significant and demonstrable bearing on the matter at hand: affording evidence tending to prove or disprove the matter at issue or under-discussion".[176] The initial request by the Carnegie and Ford Foundations to become more rigorous was an invitation to schools of management to do more than just bring examples of practice into the classroom, but to build the theoretical relevance of any given experience. In the academic world, however, scientific rigour has assumed hierarchical superiority to practice as the criteria for career development of professors of schools of management. Indicators of suboptimal outcomes in the relationship between practice and academia is that the journal rated as most prestigious academically, goes unread by practitioners. The non-cooperative game between practice and scientific observation has found Nash equilibrium in a different place than in the potentially optimal outcome of relevance. As mentioned in the first chapter of this book invitation and poison were the same word in ancient Germanic languages and in this case the Carnegie and Ford Foundation invitations turned into poison.

Medical schools, faced with a similar problem of balancing practice and rigour, have combined scientific method and observation with practice, by constructing the "teaching hospital". Today, only one business school to date has worked with the idea of scientific study on the one hand, and the exercise of practice on the other. The Cornell University School of Management has begun an MBA fund, in which students actually experiment with a real fund what they have learned about investing financial resources.[177] This is a similar model to teaching hospitals in medicine where students practice what they learn in theory.

Parallels are made with medicine, there is no such thing as surgery in theory without a capacity to practice and each can benefit from the other. Theory and practice are in a non-cooperative game of sorts, there is no third party which can force universities to collaborate with practitioners or force practitioners to appreciate the scientific rigour of universities. The optimal solution of the non-cooperative game is relevance: by observing practice it is possible to draw some larger and more scientifically rigorous conclusions; these conclusions, in turn, must bring insight to the practitioner who may be lost in "the specific example".

For example, the studies on learning curves in the operating theatre from the Harvard Business School (discussed in Chapter 2) scientifically demonstrated that surgical teams learned faster and reduced operating time and errors much more quickly than surgeons who did not work in teams. Research of this kind shows how watching surgeons practice can generate a theory of practice that, in turn, is useful to surgeons. It is from the interaction between practice on the one hand and scientific rigour in observing practice on the other that the idea of relevance or "actionable theory" proposed by the Academy of Management is born.

Practice needs a theory in order to improve itself, otherwise, alone it tends to suffer from ungrounded assumptions. The fallacies of acting on opinions rather than on rational choice were amply illustrated in Chapter 4. The following example from basketball is just another case in point.

Talent scouts seek out players and are thought to be "experts" who can find a good player with a trained eye. "Figuring whether one basketball player is better than another is a challenge similar to figuring out whether one heart surgeon is better than another: you have to find a way to interpret someone's individual statistics in the context of the team they're on and the task that they are performing."[178] What economists found in studying the criteria for selecting all-star players in basketball was that "scoring" was weighted more than any other variable in the game: stealing the ball, speed, setting up the plays, passing the ball. Scoring turns out not to be statistically correlated to winning the game.

So when economists analysed all the evidence and weighted it they discovered that Allen Iverson, Rookie of the Year, NBA all-star team player for six years running, and most valuable player in 2001, in fact ranked 91st in the league, the same year he won the "most valuable player" award. The economists set out to analyse the evidence and determine which behaviours contribute to the team winning the game. They then determine a win score which describes how the single player's contribution translates into the number of wins for the team. They discovered that the intuition that a great shooter makes for a great team player was entirely false. So Allen Iverson, with a 77 million dollar four-year contract, actually averaged for behaviours that contributed to winning games, and was not the "most valuable player".[179]

This example shows how practice without rigour creates a lack of relevance or a suboptimal result of the non-cooperative game. The authors of The Wages of Wins conclude "If you do not systematically track what the players do, and then uncover the statistical relationship between these actions and wins, you will never know why teams win and why they lose".[180]

On the contrary rigour without practice creates an equally suboptimal result. A student who learned the theory of swimming would drown in water. The same would go for playing an instrument. The quality of the faculty of schools of management, were they to be measured both on rigour and practical experience, would reveal a tendency to lean heavily towards rigour. When criticizing themselves, schools of management argue that where their faculty have no practical experience in businesses and organizations, they are not be able to identify research problems that practitioners believe are interesting, and as a result, they do not teach practitioners something useful. According to this critique, faculty members have created a new environment where they talk about the theory of running a business and this holds less and less interest to practitioners. It's as if theorists of swimming spoke to one another about the theory of swimming, while the swimmers were swimming wondering when the theorists were actually going to put a foot in the water.

The point that is made is that theory and practice are complementary and the optimal result of the non-cooperative game between them needs to be an "and" "and" not an "either" "or". There is a non-cooperative game between academia and practitioners, and this has produced a situation in which the optimal outcome is not in the same position as Nash equilibrium. Nash equilibrium in this case is that academics speak to one another, and best practice practitioners do not possess academic degrees. The optimal outcome instead lies in identifying the common interest in the question of relevance. In other words, "business school faculties simply must rediscover the practice of business".[181]

A view from the field: rigour + practice = relevance

From a communication theory perspective, the self-critique of the school of management has to do with identifying the audience. Academic management research reports and articles are losing an audience – the practitioner – the customer of the school of management – while focusing on another audience: other academics. From a theoretical perspective professionals professing scientific rigour are focusing their communication on other professionals of the same kind. Over time this generates the production of the theory of the theory. Theory of theory does not create relevance and loses students. In the self-critique the two reports identify this lack of relevance and express it in these terms: the student of the school of management should weigh the value of having acquired a period of experience over the value of investing in a period of education. If the latter is more valuable, then the school of management has truly lost its audience.[182]

Communication theory argues that all communication is directed to an audience. The audience has needs and expectations. From a practical standpoint there are many ways for schools of management to learn more about their audience and reacquire relevance in order to focus their communication. These include practice-based experiences like internships, action research, and consulting, for example. All of these practices are in no way scientifically rigorous; however, they do help theorists identify the interesting questions.

In a world where hierarchy and managerial function in the organization continue to be the most visible recognition of success, another indicator of the suboptimal outcome of the relationship between theory and practice is that most successful CEOs are not, by and large, MBA degree holders. "Our management schools have done an admirable job of training the organization's specialists – management scientists, marketing researchers, accountants and organizational development specialists. But for the most part, they have not trained managers".[183] While many CEOs are surrounded by MBA degree holders, the MBAs are not making it to the top of the organization. In Italy, most small and medium size businesses are family-owned. The founding generation generally may not have more than a high school education. The most successful US businessmen, by and large, do not possess MBA degrees.

Why schools of management are not creating managers is explained by what managers do and how they do it. In different studies that kept diaries of how managers use their time, the most interesting finding was that management is dispensed in micro units of time.[184] The average activity of the manager takes less than nine minutes. Therefore, it would appear that managers do not in fact reflect, study and interpret. It does appear that managers "ask themselves the right question". The essence of relevance is in fact, the ability to ask an interesting question.

The problem of the right question can be reframed as the problem of the "interesting question". In a recent bestseller *Freakonomics*, the following comment was made by coauthor Dubner on his coauthor Levitt:

> "As Levitt sees it, economics is a science with excellent tools for gaining answers but a serious shortage of interesting questions... For instance: if drug dealers make so much money, why do they still live with their mothers? Which is more dangerous a gun or a swimming pool?... He sifts through a pile of data to find a story that no one else has found".[185]

In *Freakonomics*, the fascinating part of the book lies in the fact that its authors ask really interesting questions and the data analysis gives interesting answers.

One example is why has there been a crime drop in US cities?

The traditional answer to this question has been new methods of policing and more police officers. However these explanations reflect the intentions of the policies that were designed and enacted but can be discarded as causes of this positive outcome when the data on crime is analysed. The data on crime rates show that murders dropped in all cities, even where no new policemen were hired and no innovative policing took place. Even more disconcerting is that these drops in crime took place before police forces were increased and innovative strategies were enacted. The authors of *Freakonomics* affirm that the drop in crime in the late nineties is directly correlated to the legalization of abortion in Roe vs. Wade, in 1973. "By 1980, the number of abortions reached 1.6 million (one for every 2.25 live births)."[186] With access to abortion, many mothers in poverty are no longer giving birth to children who then become criminals because of the hopeless social economic conditions in which they would have grown up. The strongest predictors of crime are childhood poverty and a single parent household.[187]

Freakonomics gives many fascinating examples of how analysis of the data does not confirm the hypothesis or the intent of innovation. It is interesting to see how little data seems to be used to evaluate policies and how much of policy evaluation seems to be based on "it must be" based on the intentions of policy makers in what was done about the problem. This is another way of applying the ideas of intention and perception discussed in the previous chapter. There appears to be an intention bias in evaluating policies, and little attention to measuring and understanding the why of what happened.

An example from the healthcare management realm is pharmaceutical budgets for GPs in a LHA in Italy.

The pharmaceutical budget is an attempt to contain pharmaceutical spending on the basis of the GP's case mix and an estimated cost of prescriptions based on an appropriate application of clinical guidelines. GPs received monetary incentives for meeting budget objectives. The data on pharmaceutical spending in a LHA, after the introduction of budgets for GPs, showed that GPs' yearly spending had been contained and had met budget objectives. What might be easily concluded is that budgets are an effective tool for containing spending and improving appropriateness in care.

However, a detailed look at the data showed that GPs' prescriptive behaviour remained unaltered in the first three-quarters of the year. However, in the last quarter, it dropped dramatically in those cases where the physician had over-prescribed in the first three-quarters, so that those physicians that had over-prescribed in the first part of the year almost completely curtailed prescriptions between September and December to meet budget objectives.

While LHAs appeared to be meeting target objectives, in fact spending was being contained at the expense of providing appropriate care. Only a careful *Freakonomics* approach to reading the data gives the information healthcare managers need to know.

Therefore one objective in the learning process is that students learn to be keen observers, to be "receptive" to data on the one hand and to ask the interesting question on the other.

Content and teaching method

Building the peer to peer relationship skills of students can be viewed using communication theory as a frame. As was described before, every communication contains both a content and a proposed relationship. If the necessary skill set for peer to peer efficacy is viewed exclusively as a content problem it would make sense to solve the crisis by offering specific skill building courses in all school of management products. In fact, this has already been done. Courses in strategic management, decision making, team building, and negotiation flood the catalogues of most graduate schools of management.

If these themes are viewed as both a content and a proposed relationship problem then it is of great interest to examine how the learning environment itself can create "practice". Schools of management offer a number of social conditions that are of great importance. In other words, this is known as the learning environment and it is structured by the teaching method.

Today, the structure of the learning environment in Italy is riddled with assumptions that have proven themselves false. The classroom itself is assumed to be a place in which some of the less "academic" concepts pass by osmosis. Given that the classroom meets for a year or two, it is assumed that the student will learn to listen. Given that the class is thrown together day after day, it is assumed that students learn to construct peer to peer relationships. Given that many projects are conducted as "group work", it is assumed that students learn to work in teams. Given that the students are given courses in quantitative methods, it is assumed that they use the concepts and apply them to unravelling business case studies in other courses.

Networking and building peer to peer relationships, like listening, are not skills that are passively acquired through the process itself. They need to be underlined, nurtured and evaluated, to grow expertise.

Both of these skills, peer to peer and networking, can be achieved through the teaching method. The most relevant theory in which to frame the learning process is through the literature on adult learning.

Building peer to peer relationships is both a matter of content (theory) and of proposed relationship (practice), learning happens when practice meets scientific rigour. When practice and theory are combined effectively, the relevance of the two components emerges. Relevance means we ask ourselves an interesting question. In order to struggle with relevance, from the academic side, this involves variation and experimentation with "teaching methods".

One of the primary skills that has been described as an attribute of the healthcare manager in these chapters is the capacity to observe. In other terms, this is the capacity to listen or what was described as receptivity. "The doctors have always found it necessary to take account of what patients tell them...the physician listens, first to what the patient wants to tell, secondly, for implications of what he doesn't want to tell, and thirdly for implications of what he can't tell".[188] In the field of management, the new theory of intuitive management identifies the receptivity skill in non-verbal information and its importance in asking the right question and in decision making.

An interesting story in the Buddhist religion about the capacity to observe makes a case in point:

A young man was anxious to become a Buddhist monk and study with a renowned Buddhist. He worked long and hard to merit his tutorship and finally was offered an invitation to study with this monk.

When he arrived at the temple, he was welcomed to a room with a chair and a desk. On the desk was a fish on a plate. The monk told him to observe the fish carefully and to take note of its characteristics. After 40 minutes of careful and painstaking observation, the student felt as if he had completed his task and waited impatiently for his tutor to come back. But the tutor did not return. Therefore, he deduced that he should observe more carefully. He observed the fish some more and noticed things he had not noticed before. At the end of the day, he truly expected his tutor to return, but he did not. He continued to observe new things and then satisfied with his efforts he would wait for his tutor. Since his tutor did not come back, to fill in the time, he would get back to work. He alternated observing the fish, waiting for his tutor to come back and observing the fish some more. His tutor had disappeared. Finally at the end of the week, his tutor returned and asked: Well? What did you discover? After the student gave him all of his observations collected in stops and starts during the week, the tutor said "nice beginning, keep up the good work". After three months, the student had done a thorough observation of his fish.

This story is not only a story but is a teaching method for botanists and all professions where it is of utmost importance to refine the capacity to observe. Furthermore, the analysis of the specific field of healthcare has determined the importance of reading situations, observing relationships and collecting relevant data with rigour and scientific method. Students of healthcare management need to observe the fish so that they learn to observe.

In other words, building an optimal relationship between scientific rigour and practice, develops the ability to find the relevant question. The practice side of rigour is the capacity to observe. Those who set out to describe the win factor of a player had to observe much more than the capacity to shoot baskets, they had to observe all the actions and then choose those that contributed to winning the game. They had to observe all the skills displayed by the players in basketball in order to find the relevant question which was to ask what professional competences make for a winning team?

The theory of intuitive management explored in the previous chapters is that the intuitive manager is able to "thin slice" or has the capacity to analyse a huge amount of data and to read that data for its determining characteristics in a "blink". Intuitive management describes an unconscious capacity certain managers have for observing and processing data without realizing that that is what they are doing. This capacity to observe and then to select those items worth observing, is built over time with practical experience.

The fish story is emblematic of the idea that we have to learn to observe. If we sit in a room for 40 minutes with a fish, our observations are careless and summary. Naturally, schools of management are not training Buddhists to become monks and cannot have their students observe a fish for three months, however the moral of the story is that observation is not a casual group of random elements but a methodical and complex activity that must be structured.

Observation is collected with a method. In medicine, observation is structured in what is known as the anamnesis. The word anamnesis is defined as "a recalling to mind". The power of observation when it is constructed as a method is that the physician asks the patient specific questions that permit a complete case history of the patient's situation. Being methodical about taking patient anamnesis is of great importance and this can be seen in teaching hospitals. The following example from a teaching hospital shows how observation is taught as a method. It involves a student of medicine taking the anamnesis of an 80-year old dental patient.

The student took the clip board with the questions that were to be asked. He began to read them out loud. As the patient responded, the student took note of the patient's response: age, allergies, medications, etc. When the student got to the question "are you HIV positive?", the student paused, stuttered, turned red in the face and skipped the question, mumbling to himself out loud, that given the patient's age, it was obviously not an appropriate question. As he skipped the HIV question and began to read the following question, the training physician interrupted the student and was very brusque in tone and in manner.

The training physician raised his voice: the question was there for a reason, he explained adamantly. The safety of the patient and the physician were at stake. Did the student think it was appropriate not to have this information? Was there any reason to believe that this patient had not engaged in sexually risky behaviour? Was there any reason to believe that he had not had a bad blood transfusion? Was there any reason to believe that he was not an intravenous drug user? The physician underlined that all the questions on the questionnaire must always be asked even if the patient was a nun and even if the patient was 100 years old.

The student turned even redder as he realized that observation must be methodical and is not a question of personal judgement or of stereotypes or preconceptions.

The physician must have a knowledge of diagnostic tools, but it is the anamnesis, or the capacity to observe this specific patient, that determines which of these tools will be useful in securing a definitive diagnosis. A battery of tests without a hypothesis is not an appropriate means by which to effect a diagnosis.

The school of management and the problem of observation can find many parallels to the anamnesis and the diagnosis in the school of medicine. The school of management introduces the student to analytical tools for processing observations: budgeting, quality management, risk management are all examples of analytical tools.

Management like medicine, has an observation phase, a diagnostic phase, and lastly a prescriptive phase known as change. Constructing a diagnosis is only partially a question of using the right analytical tools. Before using the tools, as was exemplified in the story of the illegal Senegalese patient described in the first chapter, the quality of the anamnesis is extremely important. The quality of the anamnesis depends on constructing a method of observation. In management the method of observation must contain both verbal and non-verbal information.

If we consider the example of excessive lengths of stay in surgery due to the relationship between the surgeon and the radiologist, then we can see that the method of observation for understanding problems must involve non-verbal and verbal clues. Without noticing the gleaming eye of the nurse, the consultant would not have discovered the reasons for excessive length of stay.

In the case of the Senegalese patient, the physician summarily observed that the patient was limping, it appeared from his gait that he had a hip problem, so an x-ray was done and when that was inconclusive, a bone biopsy was prescribed. These were not methodical observations. Instead, a complete anamnesis would have revealed that the real problem was a sexually transmitted disease and an antibiotic was an appropriate response.

As good medicine depends on careful and methodological observation, good management also depends on observation as a method not as a random series of things that are striking. It is important to observe the organization and collect observations. This is the meaning of an anamnesis. A bone biopsy is an analytical tool but using it without having fully observed the case is costly and does not produce an outcome. Likewise in an organization with a pathology, not all management tools are useful for all problems, but need to be chosen to best respond to the anamnesis of the organization.

Relevance depends on the capacity to observe, and observation is a methodical task. From methodical observation, it is possible to ask an interesting question. A solid methodical approach to observation helps students find the relevant question. Only later does finding the right analytical tool, and then problem solving enter the process.

The fish in the school of management is a metaphor for the case study method. The case study is the fish. The analysis of the case study is the capacity to observe the fish. The Harvard Business School Method suggests that there should be no impositions on how to observe the fish. No questions to answer, no constrictions. The student can choose to observe it alone or in groups. The original Harvard Case Study Method was designed with the following rules: the students were asked to read the case and prepare the analysis before coming to class. The case presented a situation but did not ask a question. Students could work alone or in groups as they preferred. The idea was the student would discover that studying alone rendered the observations less acute than those who had studied in groups. Over time, the method argued, the student would self-determine that it was more effective to work in groups, so they would not be forced to work in groups but would choose to. The instructor was a facilitator and was there to stimulate the debate. There were no "teaching notes" or "right answers".

Another approach, more frequently found in Europe, on the other hand, uses the case study as a group assignment. Studying in groups is seen as a way of learning to work in teams. By assigning cases to be analysed and presented by a group, theoretically a training ground for building peer to peer relationships is created. Study guide questions are distributed to direct the discussion and teaching notes are used to keep track of the "moral of the story": there is a pre-existing menu of what the student is supposed to learn from the case. It also gives schools of management a greater possibility to control the quality of materials and messages that are brought into the classroom.

This adaptation of the case study method does three things: it requires students to work in groups, it asks the questions for the group and it has "an answer". These rules influence the behaviour of the students.

Students are responding to someone else's question. Students also know that there is already an answer. So their focus is on getting the right answer. The group substitutes the goal of learning to observe and do a full anamnesis with the goal of using analytical tools to give the right answer. In other words, the ability to create relevance which begins with careful observation, is skipped in favour of using tools to grope for the right answer.

As *Freakonomics* points out, the interesting story comes out of the capacity to observe. As groups search for the right answer, the group tends to obliterate attention to details in the case itself and attribute value to theoretical "solutions".

Proposals for building blended peer to peer skills

The proposal is that executive education and master programs find a new balance. As things stand the emphasis is on using analytical tools to find a moral in the story, that is, the right answer. The proposal is that there be a balance between learning the analytical tools and learning to observe, building peer to peer relationships and asking good questions. In other words, returning to the metaphor provided by medicine, the focus right now is on learning to use diagnostic tests, and to prescribe medication, while there is almost no emphasis on the anamnesis or creating a hypothesis for a good question (*which diagnostic tools should I use*). The teaching is focused on what to know and abandons the issue of how to act. In the words of Arthur Stone Dewing, one of the founders of the case study method: "[managers must be able] to meet in action the problems arising out of new situations of an ever-changing environment. Education accordingly, would consist of acquiring facility to act in the presence of new experience. It asks not how a man may be trained to know, but how a man may be trained to act".[189]

There needs to be variety in teaching methods, and a balance that favours both learning to know (use analytical tools and problem solve) with learning to act (observe, build horizontal relationships and ask questions). As the analytical and prescriptive parts of the teaching method are well managed with frontal lessons and the adaptation of the Harvard Case Study Method to include study guide questions and teaching notes, the focus of this chapter will be on the other half of the balance, the part where classroom time is used to develop peer to peer skills, rational choice language for peer to peer communication and a good question. This is the part where the objective of the school of management is to develop "dependable self-reliance" in the student.[190]

Action

From a practical standpoint, what needs to be done in order to develop dependable self-reliance is to rebalance the school of management teaching process by shifting the spotlight from the professor to the student. Student-centred development is described here as a self-study design model which furnishes students with access to experts and facilitators. The professor, in this model, directs students only in as much as the role offers expertise in accumulated experience in the field and in where to look for practical information. The student experiences peer to peer relationships, evidenced-based discussions, self-study methods. The objectives of the teaching method are to encourage the student to observe and ask good questions. The purpose of these learner-centred teaching methods is to develop dependable self-reliance and the capacity to act.

In order to work towards introducing new learning experiences in the school of management teaching method, three models for achieving these are proposed: distance learning, the original Harvard Case Study Method and self study design in groups. These are just three examples of methods that already exist and that develop either directly or indirectly, the student's ability to observe, integrate horizontally, use the language of rational choice and ask a good question. In the words of Alfred North Whitehead: "What the faculty have to cultivate is activity in the presence of knowledge. What the students have to learn is activity in the presence of knowledge. This discussion rejects the doctrine that students should first learn passively, and then, having learned, should apply knowledge".[191]

Distance learning

The distance learning method uses technology to create a virtual learning environment.

Distance learning methods are designed to accommodate the following learning needs: people who have little or no time to attend classes during university business hours, a network of resources that allow the student to participate in a classroom that is not limited to the four walls of a room and the people sitting in it, and a form of communication that allows for all exchanges to be recorded and therefore observed more than just in real time.

Distance learning requires students to participate in "class discussions" in forums. Forums occur in deferred time so if a participant is available to study at 4 in the morning there are no restrictions as to when exactly participants are to be involved in the discussion. Participants have never seen one another so that fellow classmates could be an investment banker, a housefather, a mother of six children or a gardener. The relationship between classmates is focused on content, and participants are asked to discuss issues in a common language, that of rational choice.

The classroom itself has no boundaries because if students raise interesting questions about the reading they have done, these are sent by the instructor to the author of the reading for comments. Therefore the classroom is a network of learners and a network of professors. This is extremely important as a metaphor for the importance of horizontal integration in organization. Professors who do not teach in the university are voluntarily responding to student questions and needs. It is a working example of the Linux or "open source" horizontal integration mechanism. The following anecdote explains the origin of the open source horizontal integration mechanism.

Unix was an operating system designed by AT&T. One programmer, Linus Trovald, decided that it could be done better if good programmers wherever they may have been working or living, contributed to make a better product. He made his own modifications and put it online inviting anyone who was interested to contribute to its development. This became known as the "open source movement" and the Linux product (after Linus the open source originator) is considered as good as its proprietary Unix rival.[192]

The distance learning experience can create an open source classroom, and by doing so demonstrate the utility and effectiveness of the horizontal integration mechanism across organizational boundaries. The possibility for the professor to facilitate exchanges between the authors on the reading list and the learning environment enriches the student's academic experience but also shows students how important relationships are and how they can cross the boundaries of organizations to achieve results.

Forums for working in groups allow students to work in deferred time and the "written word" enables the student to reflect on relationship management. Furthermore, instructors and tutors are available to guide student learning about relationships and groups. Though it would appear that online learning would take away the non-verbal parts of expression, in fact, online culture has translated these. One recent experience concerns an instructor who in responding to a student query, left the CAPS LOCK button on by mistake. The student responded "why are you shouting at me?"

Critics of distance learning and studies of telework in general suggest that the social isolation of this form of participation is detrimental to the mental health of the participant in the long run because people need to see and meet other people. However, studies of telework in specific have found that partial telework (a combination of distance and on-site) is an extremely successful formula. Workers come to the office once a week. Likewise many distance learning programs have some encounters on-site. In the case of rebalancing the learning environment, the suggestion is that this type of learning be a part of the larger learning process but not the only part.

Harvard Case Study Method

In order to facilitate horizontal integration skills, where case studies are used, professors may consider returning to the original case method format: cases given without providing study questions, working in groups is not mandatory but a competitive advantage, and professors are there to facilitate the discussion not to reveal the right answer.

In developing this method, the class is a partnership. There are shared responsibilities for teaching and learning and the teaching requires that the professor manage both the content that is being discussed and the process of learning.[193] This is described as the "art" of managing a learning environment. "The key to effective discussion leadership is the instructor's artistry, which consists primarily of mastering detail".[194]

Using case studies enables the student to observe a range of organizations and situations. These observations allow the student to emerge from the specific experience accumulated (practice) to identify problems and issues that are relevant enough to apply not only to their experience but to be significant issues that cross organizational boundaries. The case study, not in and of itself, but as a teaching method, attempts to use many case studies to bridge the realm of practice with that of rigour and create relevance. It is not then the single case that claims relevance, it is the case method, composed of a number of cases, that claims to help the student bridge practice with rigour and identify themes of relevance.

One of the purposes of the case study method is that the student identify the competitive advantage given by horizontal integration with peers. By comparing the individual response and its breadth and depth with that of fellow students it is possible to identify the limits of the individual in the organization, and to accept that cooperation is a competitive advantage.[195]

Lastly, dependable self-reliance is developed as students come to recognize that management problems do not have a one and only one right answer but may have more than one sustainable response. The role of the professor as the facilitator who can offer students guidance in the process of learning and be a resource for accumulated knowledge helps the student develop self-reliance.

The single student in the process is asked to act, and in the process of acting, the importance of blended peer to peer relationships with other students, the language of rational choice, and the importance of a good question are revealed. An overall measure of efficacy of this partnership is that the number of student to student interactions and student to instructor initiated discussions overwhelm the number of instructor to student initiated interactions.[196]

Self-study Design

Those who have studied the learning process in adults have observed that adults learn by formulating and answering their own questions rather than having an instructor do the work for them. The instructor in this model has the objective of making sure that the advantage of accumulated knowledge is conserved, that is to make sure that students do not start again from the beginning of a question that has been answered already or that has proved of little interest. The instructor however at no time "gives a lecture" or poses a question. The instructor helps the self-study group identify the interesting question by providing them access to the accumulated knowledge in the field.

This learning method developed in continuing medical education around the problems and issues of evidence-based medicine. Traditional lectures and conferences in the pilot schools, Mc Master in Canada, Oxford in the UK were substituted by roundtables of participants. Participants were supported by two facilitators. There was a blank timetable and a flip chart. Participants first discussed and agreed upon what they needed to know and then decided how they were going to learn it.[197]

These types of programs known in executive education as self-managed forums or discussion with equivalents (peers) in other organizations received the highest ratings in the Said Business School report. 50% of executives gave it a top rating for improving personal effectiveness and 48% for improving the contribution to the organization.

These forums, by placing participants in self-managed discussions, have enabled participants to identify that decisions are made about cases based on the "opinion" or a generalization of one physician on the basis of his/her non-representative experience or on the basis of creating a "personal" algorithm. The setting needs to be conducive to identifying the learning objectives of the group. What better way to establish the importance of rational choice and its language than in having participants themselves identify the value of evidence? What better way to learn about quantitative methods than with self-directed learning questions and facilitators?

The purpose of self-managed forums is to support healthcare managers while they investigate the characteristics of winning and losing teams, and use the evidence, not opinions and personal algorithms to get results. Healthcare management and evidence-based medicine have a great deal in common: scientific rigour on the one hand, and integrating the patient perspective, on the other. "Decisions about tests and treatments should be made on the basis of mathematical estimates of their respective risks and benefits for the patient. These estimates, in turn, should be derived from a rigorous and thorough assessment of the research literature and the incorporation of all relevant values".[198]

Conclusions

This book has explored and described the specific qualities of the healthcare management environment. Managerial expertise in healthcare has been described as the capacity to obtain an optimal solution in the non-cooperative game, to build peer to peer relationships, to build trust, to exercise rational choice, to apply probability, to listen to and collect verbal and non-verbal information and to pose interesting questions. Peer to peer relationships follow patterns of dysfunction and require specific skills on the one hand and practice on the other, to be managed effectively.

In order to develop this skill set, the school of management could focus on developing the learning environment in partnership with the teaching model based on frontal lessons, syllabus and readings. Some existing examples of learning-focused teaching methods include distance learning, the original Harvard Case Study Method, and self-study evidence-based management groups. These are presented as examples of how to use the learning environment and rebalance it to focus on building the skill set for acting as a healthcare manager.

This book has collected the evidence to demonstrate that relationships with peers in the organization follow patterns of dysfunction, and are not by and large personal character conflicts. These failures are systematic. By identifying the patterns of suboptimal outcomes, it is possible to identify the optimal outcome and consequently manage these relationships. It is also possible to learn to identify patterns of relationships and to act accordingly to manage blended peer to peer relationships in the organization.

Schools of management can direct the non-cooperative debate between scientific rigour and practice to its optimal outcome: giving students a relevant exposure both in theory and in practice to building blended peer to peer relationships. Specifically, by working with and varying teaching methods, students can use the learning environment to build their management skills.

In conclusion, the spirit of this book for theorists and practitioners in healthcare management alike is captured by the words of Joseph Brodsky:

"In a manner of speaking, we all work for a dictionary. Because literature is a dictionary, a compendium of meanings for this or that human lot, for this or that experience. It is a dictionary of the language in which life speaks to man. Its function is to save the next man, a new arrival, from falling into an old trap, or to help him realize, should he fall into that trap anyway, that he has been hit by a tautology. This way he will be less impressed – and, in a way, more free. For to know the meaning of life's terms, of what is happening to you, is liberating ... if we want to play a bigger role, the role of a free man, then we should be capable of accepting – or at least imitating – the manner in which a free man fails. A free man, when he fails, blames nobody."[199]

Notes

1 Lewin, K (1951) Field theory is Social Science: selected theoretical papers. Cartwright, D (ed.) New York: Harper and Row: 169.
2 Hammer, M and Champy, J (1993) *Reengineering the Corporation.* New York: HarperCollins Publishers.
3 Idem.
4 Champy, J (1995) *Reengineering Management.* New York: Harper Business.
5 Taylor, FW (1911) *The Principles of Scientific Management.* New York: Harper.
6 Oppenheimer, T. Schooling the imagination. *Atlantic Monthly,* 1999; 284(3): 71–83.
7 Mauss, M (1967) Forms and Functions of Exchange in Archaic Societies. The Gift. New York: WW Norton: 11.
8 Normann, R (1991) Service Management. Strategy and Leadership in Service Business. New York: John Wiley: 107.
9 Landau, J, Ceda, C and DiMeana, F (2006) Reconstructing Continuity of Care in a Local Health Authority in Italy: putting humpty dumpty back together again. In Casebeer, A, Harrison, A and Mark, AL (eds) *Innovations in Health Care: A Reality Check.* London: Palgrave Macmillan.
10 Butera, F (1990) *Il Castello e la rete.* Milan: Franco Angeli.
11 Peter, LJ and Hull, R (1969) *The Peter Principle: why things always go wrong.* New York: William Morrow and Company.
12 Hurley, D. On Crime as a Science (a neighbor at a time). *The New York Times:* January 6 2004.
13 Sontag, S (1989) *Illness as a Metaphor, and AIDS and Its Metaphors.* New York: Picador.
14 Smith, R, Hiatt, H and Berwick, D. Shared ethical principles for everybody in health care: a working draft from the Tavistock Group. *BMJ.* 1999; 318: 248–51.
15 French, JPR Jr. and Raven, B (1960) The bases of social power. In Cartwright, D and Zander, A (eds) *Group dynamics.* New York: Harper and Row: 607–23.
16 Weiss, BD (2003) *Health Literacy: a manual for clinicians.* AMA Foundation.
17 Kirsh, I, Jungeblut, A, Jenkins, L and Kolstad, A (1993) Adult Literacy in America: a first look at the results of the National Adult Literacy Survey. Washington DC: National Center for Education Statistics, US Dept. of Education.
18 Williams, MV, et al. Inadequate functional health literacy among patients at two public hospitals. *JAMA.* 1995; 274: 1677.
19 Parikh, NS, et al. Shame and health literacy: the unspoken connection. *Patient Education and Counseling.* 1996; 27: 33–9.
20 Bremner, AD. Antihypertensive medication and quality of life – silent treatment of a silent killer. *Cardiovascular Drugs and Therapy.* 2002; 16: 353–64.

21 Monane, M, et al. Non Compliance with Congestive Heart Failure Therapy in the Elderly. *Archives and Internal Medicine.* 1994; 154: 433–7.

22 Racket, DL and Snow, JG (1979) The Magnitude of compliance and non compliance. In Hynes, RB, Taylor, DW and Sackett, DL (eds) *Compliance in Healthcare.* Baltimore: Johns Hopkins University Press: 11–23.

23 Goldman, L and Ausiello, D (eds) (2004) *Cecil Textbook of Medicine,* 22nd edition. Philadelphia: WB Saunders.

24 Groopman, J. Sick with worry. *The New Yorker:* August 11 2003.

25 Lemonick, MD. How to heal a hypochondriac. *Time* 2003; 162 (14): 54.

26 Groopman, J. Sick with worry. *The New Yorker:* August 11 2003.

27 Potter, ED. Medical Malpractice litigation raises health care cost, reduces access and lowers quality of care. *Issue Backgrounder.* June 19 2003: 1–9.

28 Eastaugh, SR. Reducing litigation costs through better patient communication. *The Physician Executive.* May–June 2004.

29 Beckman, HB, et al. The doctor-patient relationship and malpractice: lessons from plaintiff depositions. *Archives and Internal Medicine.* 1994; 154: 1365–70.

30 Vincent, C, Young, M and Phillips, A. Why do people sue doctors? A study of patients and relatives taking legal action. *Lancet.* 1994; 343: 1609–13.

31 Hickson, GB, et al. Factors that prompted families to file medical malpractice claims flowing perinatal injuries. *JAMA.* 1992; 267: 1359–63.

32 Watzlawick, P, Bavelas, JB and Jackson, DD (1967) *Pragmatics of Human Communication.* New York: WW Norton: 68–9.

33 Husebo, S (1997) Communication, autonomy and hope. In Surbone, A and Zwitter, M (eds) *Communication with the cancer patient: information and trust.* New York: Annals New York Academy of Sciences: 448.

34 Webster's Ninth New Collegiate Dictionary (1983) Boston MA: Miriam Webster.

35 Groopman, J. A Great Case. *New England Journal of Medicine.* 2004; 351: 20.

36 Biro, D (2000) *One hundred days, my unexpected journey from doctor to patient.* New York: Pantheon Books.

37 Groopman, J. A Great Case. *New England Journal of Medicine.* 2004; 351: 20.

38 Sontag, S (1989) *Illness as a Metaphor, and AIDS and Its Metaphors.* New York: Picador: 64.

39 Idem: 65.

40 Moja, EA e Vegni, E. La medicina centrata sul paziente. *Annali Italiani di Medicina Interna.* 1998; 13: 56–64.

41 Levenstein, JH, et al. The patient centred clinical method. *Family Practice.* 1986; 3: 24–30.

42 Campos, H (1984) La assistencia Integral al Paciente Oncologico. In Kaufmann, AE (ed.) Cancer y Sociedad, un enfoque integral. Madrid: Mezquita.

43 Husebo, S (1997) Communication, autonomy and hope. In Surbone, A and Zwitter, M (eds) *Communication with the cancer patient information and trust.* New York: Annals New York Academy of Sciences: 449.

44 Idem: 449.

45   Groopman, J. Physician Writers. *The Lancet.* 2004; 363: 88.
46   Chesney, MA. Compliance how physicians can help. *HIV Newsline,* June 1997.
47   Bull, et al. Scientific, ethical and logistical considerations in introducing a new operation: a retrospective cohort study from paediatric cardiac surgery. *British Medical Journal.* 2000; 320: 1168–73.
48   Pisano, GP, Bohmer, RMJ and Edmondson, AC. Organizational differences in rates of learning: evidence from the adoption of minimally invasive cardiac surgery. *Management Science.* 2001; 4(6): 752–68.
49   Idem: 765.
50   Gawande, A. The Bell Curve. *The New Yorker:* Dec 6 2004: 82–91.
51   Idem: 88–9.
52   Idem: 88–9.
53   Husebo, S (1997) Communication, autonomy and hope. In Surbone, A and Zwitter, M (eds) *Communication with the cancer patient information and trust.* New York: Annals New York Academy of Sciences: 443–4.
54   Idem: 447.
55   Gul, F. A nobel prize for game theorists: the contributions of Harsanyi, Nash and Selten. *Journal of Economic Perspectives.* 1997; II (3): 159–74.
56   Von Neumann, J and Morgenstern, O (1947) *The theory of games and economic behaviour.* Princeton NJ: Princeton University Press: 147–8.
57   Kovner, AR (1989) Health Services Management. A book of cases. 3rd Edition. Ann Arbor Michigan: Health Administration Press: Chapter 14: A personal experience of hospitalization.
58   Luce, DR and Raiffa, H (1957) *Games and decisions.* New York: John Wiley.
59   Von Damme, E and Weibull, JW. Equilibrium in strategic interaction: the contributions of John C Harsanyi, John F Nash and Reinhard Selten. *Scandinavian Journal of Economics.* 1995; 97 (1).
60   Nash, J (1950) unpublished thesis.
61   Myerson, RB. Nash Equilibrium and the History of Economic Theory. *Journal of Economic Literature.* 1999; XXXVII: 1067–82.
62   Landau, J and Brambilla, A. La medicina di gruppo a Milano e provincia: i reali contenuti. *Mecosan.* 2001; 37: 96–9.
63   Fisher, R and Ury, W (1983) *Getting to yes: negotiating agreement without Giving in.* New York: Penguin Books.
64   Friedman, J. A noncooperative equilibrium for supergames. *Review of Economic Studies.* 1971; 38: 1–12.
65   Gul, F. A nobel prize for game theorists: the contributions of Harsanyi, Nash and Selten. *Journal of Economic Perspectives.* 1997; 11 (3): 170.
66   Selten, R. Reexamination of the perfectness concept for equilibrium points in extensive games. *International Journal of Game Theory.* 1975; 4: 1–2, 25–55.
67   Rotter, J. Generalized expectancies for interpersonal trust. *American Psychologist.* 1971; 26: 444.
68   Webster New Collegiate Dictionary (1983). Boston MA: Miriam Webster.
69   Smyth, HW (1926) *Prometheus Bound,* Cambridge: Harvard University Press.
70   Gambetta, D (ed.) (1998) *Making and breaking co-operative relations.* Oxford: Blackwell.

71 Gilson, L. Trust and the development of health care as a social institution. *Social Science and Medicine.* 2003; 56: 1453–68.

72 Dasgupta, P (1989) La fiducia come bene economico. In Gambetta, D (ed.) *Le strategie della fiducia*, Milan: Einaudi: 66–7.

73 Bhattacharya, R, Devinney, TM and Pillutla, MM. A formal model of trust based on outcomes. *Academy of Management Review.* 1998; 23 (3): 460.

74 Elangovan, AR and Shapiro, D. Betrayal of trust in organizations. *Academy of Management Review.* 1998; 23 (3): 547.

75 Kivimaki, M, et al. Sickness absence in hospital physicians: 2 year follow up study on determinants. *Occupational and Environmental Medicine.* 2001; 58: 361–6.

76 McCue, MT. I'm losing my patience. *Managed Healthcare Executive.* February 2005: 19–22.

77 Firth-Cozens, J. Organizational trust: the keystone to patient safety. *Quality and Safety in Health Care.* 2004; 13: 57.

78 Columbia Action Investigation Board. Volume 1. August 2003; 97–120.

79 Elangovan, AR and Shapiro, D. Betrayal of trust in organizations. *Academy of Management Review.* 1998; 23 (3): 552.

80 Firth-Cozens, J. Organizational trust: the keystone to patient safety. *Quality and Safety in Health Care.* 2004; 13: 56–7.

81 Kleiner, A. Karin Stephenson's quantum theory of trust. Fieldnotes. January 2005; (8): 1–9.

82 Leape, LL, et al. Promoting patient safety by preventing medical error. *Journal of the American Medical Association.* 1998; 280: 1444.

83 Hall, M, et al. Trust in physicians and medical institutions. Does it matter? *Milbank Quarterly.* 2001; 79 (4): 613–39.

84 Calnan, MW and Rowe, R. Trust in Healthcare, an agenda for future research. *Nuffield Trust Seminar:* November 17 2004.

85 Calnan, MW and Sanford, E. Public trust in health care: the system or the doctor? *Quality and Safety in Health Care.* 2004; 13: 92–7.

86 Straten, GFM, et al. Public trust in Dutch health care. *Social Science and Medicine.* 2002; 55: 227–34.

87 Idem: 234.

88 Idem: 228.

89 Tarricone, R. Cost-of-illness analysis. What room is health economics? *Health Policy.* 2006; 77 (1): 51–63.

90 Bendor, J and Simon, HA. Political Science. *Political Scientist Annual Review.* 2003; 6: 433–71.

91 Gladwell, M (2005) *Blink.* New York: Little Brown and Company: 144.

92 Dawes, RM (1998) *Rational choice in an uncertain world.* Florida: Harcourt Brace Jovanovich.

93 Idem.

94 Dawes, RM (1988) *Rational choice in an uncertain world.* Florida: Harcourt Brace Jovanovich.

95 Hastie, R and Dawes, RM (2001) *Rational choice in an uncertain world: the psychology of judgement and decision making.* California: Sage Publications.

96 Idem.

97 Dawes, RM (1988) *Rational choice in an uncertain world.* Florida: Harcourt Brace Jovanovich: 227.

98   Idem: 206–7.
99   Brodsky, J (1995) *On grief and reason.* New York: Farrar Straus and Giroux.
100 Gladwell, M (2005) *Blink.* New York: Little Brown and Company: 14.
101 Idem: 40.
102 Rice, B. How plaintiff's lawyers pick their targets. *Medical Economics:* April 24 2000.
103 Levinson, W, et al. Physician patient Communication: the relationship with malpractice claims among primary care physicians and surgeons. *Journal of the American Medical Association.* 1997; 277 (7): 553–9.
104 Nalini, A, et al. Surgeon's tone of voice. A clue to malpractice history. *Surgery.* 2002; 132 (1): 5–9.
105 Gladwell, M (2005) *Blink.* New York: Little Brown and Company: 33.
106 Gladwell, M (2005) *Blink.* New York: Little Brown and Company.
107 Goldman, L, et al. Prediction of the need for intensive care in patients who come to Emergency Departments with acute chest pain. *New England Journal of Medicine.* 1996; 307 (23): 1498–504.
108 Reilly, BR, et al. Triage of patients with chest pain in the Emergency Department: a comparative study of Physicians' decisions. *American Journal of Medicine.* 2002; 112 (2): 95–103.
109 Reilly, BR, et al. Impact of a clinical decision rule on hospital triage of patients with suspected acute cardiac ischemia in the Emergency Department. *Journal of the American Medical Association.* 2002; 288: 342–50.
110 Eckman, P (2003) *Emotions revealed. Recognizing faces and feelings to improve communication and emotional life.* New York: Times Books.
111 Dawes, RM (1988) *Rational choice in an uncertain world.* Florida: Harcourt Brace Jovanovich: 208.
112 Dawes, RM (1988) *Rational choice in an uncertain world.* Florida: Harcourt Brace Jovanovich.
113 Idem.
114 Hart, S. An interview with Robert Aumann. *Macroeconomic Dynamics.* 2005; 5: 683–740.
115 Idem.
116 Altman, LK. Nobel came after years of battling the system. *New York Times:* October 11 2005.
117 Eckman, P (2003) *Emotions revealed, recognizing faces and feeling to improve communication and emotional life.* New York: Times Books.
118 Reis, LA, et al. (eds) SEER Cancer Statistics Review, 1975–2000, National Cancer Institute. Bethesda, MD (Accessed June 23 2003 at http://seer.cancer.gov/csr/1975_2000, 2003. 5 yr relative survival rates 1992–1999).
119 Cella, D, et al. Advances in quality of life measurements in oncology patients. *Seminars in Oncology.* 2002; 29 (8): 60–8.
120 Khayat, D. Changes in perception of the unwanted effects of cancer chemotherapy: fatigue is becoming the new frontier. *Drugs of Today.* 2002; 38 (1): 69–77.
121 Sprangers, MAG. Quality of life assessment in oncology – achievements and challenges. *Acta Oncologica.* 2002; 41 (3): 229–37.

122   Soni, MK and Cella, D. Quality of Life and symptom measures in onco-
       logy: an overview. *American Journal of Managed Care.* 2002; 8 (18 suppl):
       S560–73.
123   Kaplan, RM. Quality of Life: an outcomes perspective. *Archives of Physical
       Medicine and Rehabilitation.* 2002; 83 (2): 44–50.
124   Tamburini, M, Casali, P and Miccinesi, G. Outcome assessment in cancer
       management. *Surgical Clinics of North America.* 2000; 80 (2): 471–86.
125   Kiebert, G, et al. Practice and policy of measuring quality of life and
       health economics in cancer clinical trials: a survey among co-operative
       trial groups. *Quality of Life Research.* 2001; 9: 1073–80.
126   Szucs, TD. The growing importance of cost-effectiveness in oncologic
       practice. *Current Opinion in Oncology.* 1998; 10: 279–83.
127   Angell, M (2004) The truth about Drug Companies. New York: Random
       House.
128   Bottomley, A (2001) Assessment of Fatigue in cancer patients. In
       Marty, M and Pecorelli, S (eds) *Fatigue and Cancer.* Amsterdam: Elsevier:
       111–24.
129   Portenoy, RK and Itri, LM (2001) Evaluating and managing cancer related
       fatigue. In Marty, M and Pecorelli, S (eds) *Fatigue and Cancer.* Amsterdam:
       Elsevier: 21.
130   Riley III, JL, et al. Racial/ethnic differences in the experience of chronic
       pain. *Pain.* 2002; 100: 291–8.
131   Juarez, G, Ferrell, B and Borneman, T. Cultural considerations in edu-
       cation for cancer pain management. *Journal of Cancer Education.* 1999;
       14: 168–73.
132   Wan, GJ, et al. The impact of socio-cultural and clinical factors on
       health-related quality of life reports among Hispanic and African
       American cancer patients. *Journal of Outcome Measurement.* 1999; 3:
       200–15.
133   Langer, G. About Response Rates some unresolved questions. *Public
       Perspective.* 2003; May–June.
134   Mariolis, P. AAPOR 2002 Conference. "Response Rates and Data
       Accuracy".
135   Martin, CL. The impact of topic interest on mail survey response
       behavior. *Journal of the Market Research Society.* 1994; 36 (4): 327–37.
136   Curt, GA, et al. Impact of cancer-related fatigue on the lives of
       patients: new findings from the Fatigue Coalition. *Oncologist.* 2002; 5 (5):
       353–60.
137   Curt, GA. The impact of fatigue on patients with cancer: overview of
       FATIGUE 1 and 2. *Oncologist.* 2000; 5 (2): 9–12.
138   Curt, G and Johnston, PG. Cancer fatigue: the way forward. *Oncologist.*
       2003; 8 (1): 27–30.
139   Portenoy, RK and Itri, LM. Cancer related fatigue. Guidelines for evalua-
       tion and management. *Oncologist.* 1999; 4 (1): 1–10.
140   Barrier, PA, Li, JT and Jensen, NM. Two words to improve physician-
       patient communication: what else? *Mayo Clinic Proceedings.* 2003; 78 (2):
       211–14.
141   Stevenson, AC. Compassion and patient-centred care. *Australian Family
       Physician.* 2002; 31 (12): 1103–6.

142   Dowsett, SM, et al. Communication styles in the cancer consultation: preferences for a patient-centred approach. *Psycho-Oncology*. 2000; 9: 147–55.

143   Roter, D and Stewart, M (eds) (1986) *Communicating with medical patients*. London: Sage.

144   Frost, MH, Bonomi, AE and Ferrans, CE. Patient, clinician, and population perspectives on determining the clinical significance of quality of life scores. *Mayo Clinic Proceedings*. 2002; 77 (5): 488–94.

145   Brown, J, et al. The patient-centred clinical method. 2. Definition and application. *Family Practice*. 1986; 3 (2): 75–9.

146   Levenstein, JH, et al. The patient-centred clinical method. 1. A model for the doctor-patient interaction in family medicine. *Family Practice*. 1986; 3: 24–30.

147   Fortin, AH. Communication skills to improve patient satisfaction and quality of care. *Ethnicity and Disease*. 2002; 16: 80–2.

148   Levine, C (ed.) (2000) *Always on Call*. New York: United Hospital Fund: 148.

149   Watzlawick, P, Bavelas, JB and Jackson, DD (1967) *Pragmatics of Human Communication*. New York: WW Norton: 20.

150   Gladwell, M. Million Dollar Murray: why problems like homelessness may be easier to solve than to manage. *The New Yorker*: February 13 & 20 2006; 101.

151   Idem.

152   Burns, T (1990) Mechanistic and Organismic Structures. In Pugh, DS (ed.) *Organization Selected Readings*. New York: Penguin Books: 70.

153   Mintzberg, H (1990) Management and decision making. In Pugh, DS (ed.) *Organization Selected Readings*. New York: Penguin Books: 225.

154   Hammer, M and Stanton, S (1995) *The Reengineering Revolution*. New York: Harper Business.

155   Kovner, AR and Channing, AH (1994) *Really Trying. A career guide for the health services manager*. Michigan: Health Administration Press: 74–5.

156   The amputee coalition of America and the Center for Disease Control.

157   Hersey, P, Blanchard, K and Natemeyer, W (1979) *Situational Leadership, perception and the impact of power*. La Jolla, CA: Center for Leadership Studies, Learning Resources Corp.

158   Edelstein, C. Shinui ovvero cambiamento: professionalità, etica e azione politica? http://www.shinui.it /htm/articolo.

159   Gladwell, M. Troublemakers: What pit bulls can teach us about profiling, *The New Yorker*: February 6 2006.

160   Idem.

161   Hastie, R and Dawes, RM (2001) *Rational choice in an uncertain world: the psychology of judgement and decision making*. California: Sage Publications: xiii.

162   Dawes, R (1994) *House of Cards*. New York: The Free Press.

163   Webster Ninth New Collegiate Dictionary (1983). Boston MA: Miriam Webster.

164   Idem.

165   US Equal Employment Opportunity Commission, Title VII of the Civil Rights Act of 1964. http://www.eeoc.gov/abouteeo/overview_practices.html.

166 Idem.

167 Derman-Sparks, L and Phillips, CB (1997) *Teaching and Learning Anti-racism*. New York: Teachers College Press, Columbia University: 2.

168 Ryan, W (1976) *Blaming the Victim*. New York: Vintage Books.

169 Calavita, K. Blue jeans, rape, and the "de-constitutive" power of law. *Law and Society Review*. 2001; 35 (1).

170 Cassazione penale 1999: 2195.

171 Watzlawick, P, Bavelas, JB and Jackson, DD (1967) *Pragmatics of Human Communication*. New York: WW Norton: 56.

172 www.execed.oxford.edu.

173 www.execed.oxford.edu report page 16.

174 Bennis, WG and O'Toole, J. How business schools lost their way. *Harvard Business Review*: May 2005: 2.

175 Idem: 3.

176 Webster's Ninth New Collegiate Dictionary (1983) Boston MA: Miriam Webster.

177 Idem: 6.

178 Gladwell, M. Game theory, when it comes to athletic prowess, don't believe your eyes. *The New Yorker*. May 29 2006: 86–7.

179 Idem.

180 Berri, DJ, Schmidt, MB and Brook, SJ (2006) *The Wages of Wins*. Stanford: Stanford University Press.

181 Idem: 6.

182 Gragg, CI (1982) Because Wisdom can't be told. Harvard Business School Paper. 1982; 9-451-005: 3.

183 Mintzberg, H. The manager's job. Folklore and fact. *Harvard Business Review*. March–April 1990: 12.

184 Stewart, R (1967) *Managers and their jobs*. London: Macmillan.

185 Levitt, SD and Dubner, SJ (2005) *Freakonomics*. New York: William Morrow: ix.

186 Idem: 138.

187 Idem.

188 Henderson, LJ. Introductory lectures, Sociology 23 in unpublished papers, Baker Library Harvard Business School: 13–14.

189 Dewing, AS (1931) An introduction to the use of cases. In Cecil, EF (ed.) *The case method of instruction*. New York: McGraw Hill.

190 Cragg, CI (1982) Because Wisdom *can't be thought*. Harvard Business School Paper 9-451-005: 2.

191 Whitehead, AN (1947) Essays in Science and Philosophy. New York: Philosophical Library Inc: 218.

192 Gladwell, M. The Bakeoff, project Delta aims to create the perfect cookie. The New Yorker: September 5 2005: 126.

193 Gragg, CI (1994) Teachers also must learn. In Barnes, B, Christensen, CR and Hansen, AJ (eds) Teaching and the case method, 3rd edition. Cambridge, MA: Harvard Business School Press, 15–22.

194 Idem: 37.

195 Cragg, CI (1982) Because Wisdom *can't be taught*. Harvard Business School Paper 9-451-005: 5.

196   Teaching with cases at the Harvard Business School. In Barnes, B, Christensen, CR and Hansen, AJ (eds) Teaching and the case method, 3rd edition. Cambridge: Harvard Business School Press: 52.

197   Elwyn, G, Greenhalgh, T and Macfarlane, F (2001) *Groups: a guide to small group work in healthcare management education and research*. Abingdon UK: Radcliffe Medical Press.

198   Idem.

199   Brodsky, J (1995) *On Grief and Reason, Essay*. New York: Farrar Straus and Giroux, 33.

Bibliography

Altman, LK. Nobel came after years of battling the system. *New York Times*: October 11 2005.

Barrier, PA, Li, JT and Jensen, NM. Two words to improve physician-patient communication: what else? *Mayo Clinic Proceedings*. 2003; 78 (2): 211–14.

Beckman, HB, Markakis, KM and Suchman, AL. The doctor-patient relationship and malpractice: lessons from plaintiff depositions. *Archives of Internal Medicine*. 1994; 154: 1365–70.

Bendor, J and Simon, HA. Political Science. *Political Scientist Annual Review*. 2003; 6: 433–71.

Bennis, WG and O'Toole, J. How business schools lost their way. *Harvard Business Review*: May 2005.

Berri, DJ, Schmidt, MB and Brook, SJ (2006) *The Wages of Wins*. Stanford: Stanford University Press.

Bhattacharya, R, Devinney, TM and Pillutla, MM. A formal model of trust based on outcomes. *Academy of Management Review*. 1998; 23(3).

Biro, D (2000) *One hundred days, my unexpected journey from doctor to patient*. New York: Pantheon Books.

Bottomley, A (2001) Assessment of Fatigue in cancer patients. In Marty, M and Pecorelli, S (eds) *Fatigue and Cancer*. Amsterdam: Elsevier: 111–24.

Brodsky, J (1995) *On grief and reason*. New York: Farrar Straus and Giroux.

Brown, J, et al. The patient-centred clinical method. 2. Definition and application. *Family Practice*. 1986; 3 (2): 75–9.

Bull, et al. Scientific, ethical and logistical considerations in introducing a new operation: a retrospective cohort study from paediatric cardiac surgery. *British Medical Journal*. 2000; 320: 1168–73.

Burns, T (1990) Mechanistic and Organismic Structures. In Pugh, DS (ed.) *Organization Theory: Selected Readings*. New York: Penguin Books.

Bremner, AD. Antihypertensive medication and quality of life – silent treatment of a silent killer. *Cardiovascular Drugs and Therapy*. 2002; 16: 353–64.

Butera, F (1990) *Il Castello e la rete*. Milan: Franco Angeli.

Calavita, K. Blue jeans, rape, and the "de-constitutive" power of law. *Law and Society Review*. 2001; 35(1).

Calnan, MW and Rowe, R. Trust in Healthcare, an agenda for future research. Nuffield Trust Seminar: November 17 2004.

Calnan, MW and Sanford, E. Public trust in health care: the system or the doctor? *Qual Saf Health Care*. 2004; 13: 92–7.

Campos, H (1984) La Assistencia Integral al Paciente Oncologico. In Kaufmann, AE (ed.) *Cancer y Sociedad un enfoque integral*. Madrid: Mezquita.

Cassazione penale 1999: 2195.

Cella, D, et al. Advances in quality of life measurements in oncology patients. *Seminars in Oncology*. 2002; 29 (8): 60–8.

Chesney, MA. Compliance how physicians can help, *HIV Newsline*: June 1997.

Columbia Action Investigation Board. Volume 1. August 2003; 97–120.

Curt, GA, et al. Impact of cancer-related fatigue on the lives of patients: new findings from the Fatigue Coalition. *Oncologist.* 2002; 5 (5): 353–60.

Curt, GA. The impact of fatigue on patients with cancer: overview of FATIGUE 1 and 2. *Oncologist.* 2000; 5 (2): 9–12.

Curt, G and Johnston, PG. Cancer fatigue: the way forward. *Oncologist.* 2003; 8 (1): 27–30.

Dasgupta, P (1989) La fiducia come bene economico. In Gambetta, D (ed.) *Le strategie della fiducia*, Milano: Einaudi.

Dawes, RM (1988) *Rational choice in an uncertain world.* Florida: Harcourt Brace Jovanovich.

Dawes, R (1994) *House of Cards.* New York: The Free Press.

Derman-Sparks, L and Phillips, CB (1997) *Teaching and Learning Anti-racism.* New York: Teachers College Acts, Columbia University: 2.

Dewing, AS (1931) An introduction to the use of cases. In Cecil, EF (ed.) *The case method of instruction.* New York: McGraw Hill.

Dowsett, SM, et al. Communication styles in the cancer consultation: preferences for a patient-centred approach. *Psycho-Oncology.* 2000; 9: 147–55.

Eastaugh, SR. Reducing litigation costs through better patient communication. *The Physician Executive.* May–June 2004.

Eckman, P (2003) *Emotions revealed. Recognizing faces and feelings to improve communication and emotional life.* New York: Times Books.

Edelstein, C. Shinui ovvero cambiamento: professionalità, etica e azione politica? http://www.shinui.it/htm/articolo: accessed September 2006.

Elangovan, AR and Shapiro, D. Betrayal of trust in organizations. *Academy of Management Review.* 1998; 23 (3).

Elwyn, G, Greenhalgh, T and Macfarlane, F (2001) *Groups: a guide to small group work in healthcare management education and research.* Abingdon UK: Radcliffe Medical Press.

Firth-Cozens, J. Organisational trust: the keystone to patient safety. *Quality and Safety in Health Care.* 2004; 13 (1): 56–61.

Fisher, R and Ury, W (1983) *Getting to yes: negotiating agreement without giving in.* New York: Penguin Books.

Fortin, AH. Communication skills to improve patient satisfaction and quality of care. *Ethnicity Disease.* 2002; 16: 80–2.

French, JPR Jr. and Raven, B (1960) The bases of social power. In Cartwright, D and Zander, A (eds) *Group dynamics.* New York: Harper and Row: 607–23.

Friedman, J. A noncooperative equilibrium for supergames. *Review of Economic Studies.* 1971; 38: 1–12.

Frost, MH, Bonomi, AE and Ferrans, CE. Patient, clinician, and population perspectives on determining the clinical significance of quality of life scores. *Mayo Clinic Proceedings.* 2002; 77 (5): 488–94.

Gambetta, D (ed.) (1998) *Making and breaking co-operative relations.* Oxford. Blackwell.

Gawande, A. The Bell Curve. *The New Yorker:* December 6 2004: 82–91.

Gilson, L. Trust and the development of health care as a social institution. *Social Science and Medicine.* 2003; 56: 1453–68.

Gladwell, M (2005) *Blink.* New York: Little Brown and Company.

Gladwell, M. The Bakeoff, project Delta aims to create the perfect cookie. *The New Yorker:* September 5 2005.

Gladwell, M. Troublemakers: what pit bulls can teach us about profiling. *The New Yorker*: February 6 2006.

Gladwell, M. Million Dollar Murray: why problems like homelessness may be easier to solve than to manage. *The New Yorker*: February 13 & 20 2006.

Gladwell, M. Game Theory, when it comes to athletic prowess, don't believe your eyes. *The New Yorker*. May 29 2006.

Goldman, L and Ausiello, D (eds) (2004) *Cecil Textbook of Medicine*, 22nd edition. Philadelphia: WB Saunders.

Goldman, L, et al. Prediction of the need for intensive care in patients who come to Emergency Departments with acute chest pain. *New England Journal of Medicine*. 1996; 307 (23): 1498–504.

Gragg, CI. Because Wisdom can't be told. Harvard Business School Paper. 1982; 9-451-005.

Gragg, CI (1994) Teachers also must learn. In Barnes, B, Christensen, CR and Hansen, AJ (eds) *Teaching and the case method*. 3rd edition. Cambridge MA: Harvard Business School Press: 15–22.

Groopman, J. Sick with worry. *The New Yorker*: August 11 2003.

Groopman, J. A Great Case. *New England Journal of Medicine*. 2004; 351: 20.

Groopman, J. Physician Writers. *The Lancet*. 2004; 363: 88.

Gul, F. A nobel prize for game theorists: the contributions of Harsanyi, Nash and Selten. *Journal of Economic Perspectives*. 1997; 11 (3): 159–74.

Hall, M, et al. Trust in physicians and medical institutions. Does it matter? *Milbank Quarterly*. 2001; 79 (4): 613–39.

Hammer, M and Stanton, S (1995) *The Reengineering Revolution*. New York: Harper Business.

Hammer, M and Champy, J (1993) *Reengineering the Corporation*. New York: HarperCollins Publishers.

Hart, S. An interview with Robert Aumann. *Macroeconomic Dynamics*. 2005; 5: 683–740.

Hastie, R and Dawes, RM (2001) Rational choice in an uncertain world: the psychology of judgement and decision making. California: Sage Publications.

Henderson, LJ. Introductory lectures: Sociology 23 in unpublished papers. Baker Library Harvard Business School.

Hersey, P, Blanchard, K and Natemeyer, W (1979) Situational Leadership, perception and the impact of power. La Jolla, CA: Center for Leadership Studies, Learning Resources Corp.

Hickson, GB, et al. Factors that prompted families to file medical malpractice claims flowing perinatal injuries. *JAMA* 1992; 267: 1359–63.

Hurley, D. On Crime as a Science (a neighbor at a time). *The New York Times*: January 6 2004.

Husebo, S (1997) Communication, autonomy and hope. In Surbone, A and Zwitter, M (eds) *Communication with the cancer patient: information and trust*. New York: Annals New York Academy of Sciences.

Juarez, G, Ferrell, B and Borneman, T. Cultural considerations in education for cancer pain management. *Journal of Cancer Education*. 1999; 14: 168–73.

Kaplan, RM. Quality of Life: an outcomes perspective. *Archives of Physical Medicine and Rehabilitation*. 2002; 83 (2): 44–50.

Khayat, D. Changes in perception of the unwanted effects of cancer chemotherapy: fatigue is becoming the new frontier. *Drugs of Today*. 2002; 38 (1): 69–77.

Kiebert, G, et al. Practice and policy of measuring quality of life and health economics in cancer clinical trials: a survey among co-operative trial groups. *Quality of Life Research.* 2001; 9: 1073–80.

Kirsh, I, Jungeblut, A, Jenkins, L and Kolstad, A (1993) Adult Literacy in America: a first look at the results of the National Adult Literacy Survey. Washington DC: National Center for Education Statistics, US Dept. of Education.

Kivimaki, M, et al. Sickness absence in hospital physicians: 2 year follow up study on determinants. *Occupational and Environmental Medicine.* 2001; 58: 361–6.

Kleiner, A. Karen Stephenson's quantum theory of trust. Fieldnotes. January 2005; (8): 1–9.

Kovner, AR and Channing, AH (1994) *Really Trying. A career guide for the health services manager.* Michigan: Health Administration Press.

Kovner, AR (1989) *Health Services Management. A book of cases.* 3rd Edition. Ann Arbor Michigan: Health Administration Press.

Landau, J and Brambilla, A. La medicina di gruppo a Milano e provincia: i reali contenuti. *Mecosan.* 2001; 37: 96–9.

Landau, J, Ceda, C and DiMeana, F (2006) Reconstructing Continuity of Care in a Local Health Authority in Italy: putting humpty dumpty back together again. In Casebeer, A, Harrison, A and Mark, AL (eds) *Innovations in Health Care: A Reality Check.* London: Palgrave Macmillan.

Leape, LL, et al. Promoting patient safety by preventing medical error. *Journal of the American Medical Association.* 1998; 280: 1444.

Lemonick, MD. How to heal a hypochondriac. *Time* 2003; 162 (14): 54.

Levenstein, JH, et al. The patient-centred clinical method. *Family Practice.* 1986; 3: 24–30.

Levine, C (ed.) (2000) *Always on Call.* New York: United Hospital Fund.

Levinson, W, et al. Physician patient Communication: the relationship with malpractice claims among primary care physicians and surgeons. *Journal of the American Medical Association.* 1997; 277 (7): 553–9.

Levitt, SD and Dubner, SJ (2005) *Freakonomics.* New York: William Morrow.

Luce, DR and Raiffa, H (1957) *Games and decisions.* New York: John Wiley.

Mamet, D (1994) Oleanna: a play. Vintage Books Ed.

Mauss, M (1967) *Forms and Functions of Exchange in Archaic Societies. The Gift.* New York: WW Norton.

McCue, MT. I'm losing my patience. *Managed Healthcare Executive.* February 2005: 19–22.

Mintzberg, H (1990) Management and decision making. In Pugh, DS (ed.) *Organization Selected Readings.* New York: Penguin Books.

Mintzberg, H. The manager's job. Folklore and fact. *Harvard Business Review.* March–April 1990.

Moja, EA e Vegni, E. La medicina centrata sul paziente. *Annali Italiani di Medicina Interna.* 1998; 13: 56–64.

Monane, M, et al. Non compliance with Congestive heart failure Therapy in the Elderly. *Archives of Internal Medicine.* 1994; 154: 433–7.

Myerson, RB. Nash Equilibrium and the History of Economic Theory. *Journal of Economic Literature.* 1999; XXXVII: 1067–82.

Nalini, A, et al. Surgeon's tone of voice. A clue to malpractice history. *Surgery.* 2002; 132 (1): 5–9.

Nash, J (1950) unpublished thesis.

Normann, R (1991) *Service Management. Strategy and Leadership in Service Business.* New York: John Wiley.

Oppenheimer, T. Schooling the imagination. *Atlantic Monthly*, 1999; 284 (3): 71–83.

Parikh, NS, et al. Shame and health literacy: the unspoken connection. *Patient Education and Counseling.* 1996; 27: 33–9.

Peter, LJ and Hull, R (1969) *The Peter Principle: why things always go wrong.* New York: William Morrow and Company.

Pisano, GP, Bohmer, RMJ and Edmondson, AC. Organizational differences in rates of learning: evidence from the adoption of minimally invasive cardiac surgery. *Management Science.* 2001; 47 (6): 752–68.

Portenoy, RK and Itri, LM. Cancer related fatigue. Guidelines for evaluation and management. *Oncologist.* 1999; 4 (1): 1–10.

Portenoy, RK and Itri, LM (2001) Evaluating and managing cancer related fatigue. In Marty, M and Pecorelli, S (eds) *Fatigue and Cancer.* Amsterdam: Elsevier.

Potter, ED. Medical malpractice litigation raises health care cost, reduces access and lowers quality of care. *Issue Backgrounder.* June 19 2003: 1–9.

Racket, DL and Snow, JG (1979) The Magnitude of compliance and non compliance. In Hynes, RB, Taylor, DW and Sackett, DL (eds) *Compliance in Healthcare.* Baltimore: Johns Hopkins University Press, 11–23.

Reilly, BR, et al. Triage of patients with chest pain in the Emergency Department: a comparative study of Physicians' decisions. *American Journal of Medicine.* 2002; 112 (2): 95–103.

Reilly, BR, et al. Impact of a clinical decision rule on hospital triage of patients with suspected acute cardiac ischemia in the Emergency Department. *Journal of the American Medical Association.* 2002; 288: 342–50.

Reis, LA, et al. (eds) SEER Cancer Statistics Review, 1975–2000, National Cancer Institute. Bethesda, MD (Accessed June 23 2003 at http://seer.cancer.gov/csr/1975_2000, 2003. 5 yr relative survival rates 1992–1999).

Rice, B. How plaintiff's lawyers pick their targets. *Medical Economics.* April 24 2000.

Riley, JL, et al. Racial/ethnic differences in the experience of chronic pain. *Pain.* 2002; 100: 291–8.

Roter, D and Stewart, M (eds) (1986) *Communicating with medical patients.* London: Sage.

Roth, P (2001) The Human Stain: a novel. Vintage Books Ed.

Rotter, J. Generalized expectancies for interpersonal trust. *American Psychologist.* 1971; 26: 444.

Ryan, W (1976) *Blaming the Victim.* New York: Vintage Books.

Selten, R. Reexamination of the perfectness concept for equilibrium points in extensive games. *International Journal of Game Theory.* 1975; 4 (1): 25–55.

Smith, R, Hiatt, H and Berwick, D. Shared ethical principles for everybody in health care: a working draft from the Tavistock Group. *BMJ.* 1999; 318: 248–51.

Smyth, HW (1926) *Prometheus Bound.* Cambridge: Harvard University Press.

Soni, MK and Cella, D. Quality of Life and symptom measures in oncology: an overview. *American Journal of Managed Care.* 2002; 8 (18suppl): S560–73.

Sontag, S (1989) *Illness as a Metaphor, and AIDS and Its Metaphors*. New York: Picador.

Sprangers, MAG. Quality of life assessment in oncology – achievements and challenges. *Acta Oncologica*. 2002; 41 (3): 229–37.

Stevenson, AC. Compassion and patient-centred care. *Australian Family Physician*. 2002; 31 (12): 1103–6.

Straten, GFM, et al. Public trust in Dutch health care. *Social Science and Medicine*. 2002; 55: 227–34.

Stewart, R (1967) *Managers and their jobs*. London: Macmillan.

Szucs, TD. The growing importance of cost-effectiveness in oncologic practice. *Current Opinion in Oncology*. 1998; 10: 279–83.

Tamburini, M, Casali, P and Miccinesi, G. Outcome assessment in cancer management. *Surgical Clinics of North America*. 2000; 80 (2): 471–86.

Taylor, FW (1911) *The Principles of Scientific Management*. New York: Harper.

US Equal Employment Opportunity Commission, Title VII of the Civil Rights Act of 1964. http://www.eeoc.gov/abouteeo/overview_practices.html.

Vincent, C, Young, M and Phillips, A. Why do people sue doctors? A study of patients and relatives taking legal action. *Lancet*. 1994; 343: 1609–13.

Von Damme, E and Weibull, JW. Equilibrium in strategic interaction: the contributions of John C Harsanyi, John F Nash and Reinhard Selten. *Scandinavian Journal of Economics*. 1995; 97 (1).

Von Neumann, JV and Morgenstern, O (1947) *The theory of games and economic behavior*. Princeton NJ: Princeton University Press.

Wan, GJ, et al. The impact of socio-cultural and clinical factors on health-related quality of life reports among Hispanic and African American cancer patients. *Journal of Outcome Measurement*. 1999; 3: 200–15.

Watzlawick, P, Bavelas, JB and Jackson, DD (1967) *Pragmatics of Human Communication*. New York: WW Norton.

Webster's Ninth New Collegiate Dictionary (1983). Boston MA: Miriam Webster.

Weiss, BD (2003) *Health Literacy: a manual for clinicians*. AMA Foundation.

Whitehead, AN (1947) *Essays in Science and Philosophy*. New York: Philosophical Library Inc.

Williams, MV, et al. Inadequate functional health literacy among patients at two public hospitals. *JAMA*. 1995; 274: 1677–82.

www.execed.oxford.edu.

Index